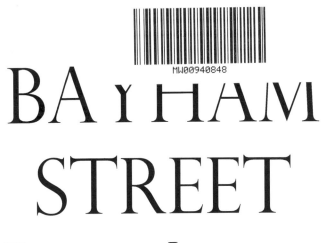

BAYHAM STREET

ESSAYS IN LONGING

Robert Clark

ALSO BY ROBERT CLARK

The Solace of Food: A Life of James Beard

River of the West

In the Deep Midwinter

Mr. White's Confession

My Grandfather's House

Love Among the Ruins

Lives of the Artists

*Dark Water: Flood and Redemption in the
City of Masterpieces*

Heaven

WWW.ROBERTCLARK.US.COM

This book is set in Perpetua, designed by
Eric Gill in 1925

Cover: *Greenwood's Map of London*, 1827

FOR PATRICIA HAMPL, DAVID SHIELDS, & GREGORY WOLFE

CONTENTS

1.

WORLDLY

When I was four or a little younger, my mother painted the den—the room at the back of the house where the television and my toys were kept—grey. It is not the first thing I remember of my childhood and scarcely the most important, but it seems to me now to mark the beginning of my education; what the German romantics would have called my formation—the making of the person I have become.

By the time I was old enough to be educated in any meaningful sense of the word—not merely to learn to talk or to behave or to perform simple tasks and recitations, but to begin to acquire a view of the world and the relative value of the things it contained—my mother, my sister, and I had been on our own for several years. My parents had divorced before I was two, and my earliest memories date from perhaps a little after that time. Those are inchoate; they lack context or narrative.

There was, for example, a large and frightening dog; and another time there was a large and frightening adult male (an elderly relative who liked to tease little boys? I can't say); and another time when I see myself sitting and then standing on the seat of a car, locked inside by myself, and outside it's winter. That's all I know, and it scarcely feels like knowing at all.

The real memories—the ones anchored by foreground and background and a palpable sense of having happened to me in the course of what seems to be the trajectory of a

life— and, it seems, my education begin around the time
my mother began painting the den.

She worked at it for some time—perhaps over the
course of a week—and she began early in the morning,
while *The Today Show* with Dave Garroway was on the TV,
and continued, after nine o'clock, when we switched to the
radio and Arthur Godfrey, whose program ran until
lunchtime. This was our routine every morning as I recall
it, whether my mother was painting or not. My sister,
being five years older than me, and at school full-time
pretty much from my infancy, doesn't really figure in it. It
was just my mother and me.

So she was painting the den grey, and you might say the
education lay in my watching her apply the paint—on a
ladder, with a roller—and in the fact that we were
connected to the wider world of Chicago and New York via
the radio and television; with Frank Blair darkly reading
teletype copy about Russian nuclear testing and satellite
launches on *Today;* and Arthur Godfrey pitching
Chesterfields (my mother's brand) on CBS, in a smoky
voice that itself seemed to smolder and fulminate; that
threatened at the end of phrases to gutter out.

But those are mere facts and experiences. What I am
trying to describe is the kind of education that forms an
understanding or at least a sensibility: a box of habits and
tools you bring to bear on the culture and society you
inhabit. And while everything—more than we can know—
surely accreted, formed the ground on which I would stand,
the crucial thing was not the TV nor the radio nor the
observation of her painting technique, but the significance,
as my mother explained to me, of her painting this color at
this moment in history. Grey, she told me more than once,
was the new, smart, fashionable, daring color; the color
that was au courant in Chicago and New York, and we were
applying it here, to our very own walls, now. Doing this, I

came to see, was not merely home maintenance or even decoration. It was exciting and it was fun, but it was more than that: it was bracing, even audacious, a leap into the world from which we had received intimations of from Garroway and Godfrey, a world that we were now making vivid and entire here on Bayard Avenue in St. Paul, Minnesota. It was, I would realize much later, a species of art.

At the time, I was also being formally educated in nursery school for a few hours a day. There was a man in a large station wagon who drove me and several other children there. The nursery school was held on the campus of a Catholic college near our neighborhood, and was taught by nuns, pre-Vatican II nuns in full habit, with wimples and rosaries and knotted cords around their waists. There was one nun I remember and whom I liked. Her name was Sister Anne, and I liked her because she liked me; and she liked me, especially (so my mother told me) because I liked—or would listen to without much fidgeting—classical music. I am pretty convinced this music was Tchaikovsky (although my mother insisted it was Beethoven), which is not so very hard to admire when you are three or four. That is all I remember about Sister Anne, that and the impression that she was small and short and perhaps rather old; although wearing a habit, I wouldn't have had much to go on, except for the face encased in the wimple and her hands at those moments when they were visible, when they emerged with a rustle from the black cocoon of her cavernous sleeves where she kept them when not in use.

I must have learned to count and to say the alphabet a little, but what sticks in my mind is the music and the nuns; or, more precisely, the shape and aura of them. And everywhere on the campus and inside the nursery school there were images of Mary—in stone, terra cotta, and plaster, on paper and canvas, hanging from the walls or placed in niches and on pedestals. The nuns were her counterparts: black where she was blue or white, but possessed of the same grave and serene presence, of formidable love and assent to God's will, a portrait of womanhood and mothering painted on a ground of silence, loss, and forbearance. The nuns were infinitely patient, and it must have been for this that I liked or at least admired them. Only many years later would I understand that the root of the word "patience" is suffering.

The nuns were not like my mother, nor would I have wanted her to be like them. Not that she did not suffer, but she scarcely forbore. She drank and smoked and laughed and commiserated with her friends. She sang along with the Broadway cast albums she played on the hi-fi, and she taught me to sing along with her.

And what is education if not imitation? While my mother painted, I watched *The Today Show* sitting on the floor behind an overturned cardboard box, in just the way that Dave Garroway sat behind his desk and chatted with the viewers; and I am pretty sure I sometimes chatted back. Garroway was one of the masters of a mellow, genial discourse that reached its apotheosis around 1950. He could talk at any length about any subject without sounding glib or trite, projecting words into space, connecting the seemingly unconnected, in a manner that was at once offhand and wise.

Two guiding principles, I think, allowed him to carry this off: first, that everything was inherently interesting; and, second, that he and we had all the time in the world. He never condescended to a subject or a person, and while he understood irony, it was untainted by suspicion or resentment. What a funny old world it was, and what better thing was there to do than look out the window and watch it go by—as indeed *The Today Show* cameras spent a considerable number of minutes doing each hour through the studio window that gave out onto the sea of hats and cloth coats passing by on the sidewalks of Rockefeller Center.

So there was the window, and with Dave behind his desk and me behind my box and the glass of the television screen between us, who was to say who was inside or outside of it? In the same mode, there were what would today considered news readings of interminable length, together with the camera's endless scan of the weather in all the towns in the nation which possessed NBC affiliates, printed by a teletype on a roll and unrolled before the static camera, known technically (and appropriately enough) as a "crawl". Seemingly anything—an image, a happenstance, the most passing of moods—would do since, as Garroway made clear and we all agreed, the mere fact of television— its very existence—was fascinating, so it scarcely mattered what was actually *on* it. The feeling was repeated, for me at least, when a dozen years later we got our first color set, and I would watch anything—not merely reruns and commercials but shows that I otherwise hated—merely to see them in color.

That was not to say that *The Today Show* of 1956 was dull or tedious, but that enjoying it was predicated on a certain good will for which we have since perhaps lost the knack: a capacity to be well-disposed towards persons or things—to assume they were well-meant and of some worth—and to give them our attention until they proved otherwise. Maybe this is innocence, but it also represents a certain confidence that the world is as it seems, that it is by at least a slight margin more good than bad, and we number ourselves among those fortunate to be in it.

That may have been the first thing I learned from life or from *The Today Show*, or perhaps it was an inclination I already possessed by way of an inherited transcendent human disposition. In any case, sitting behind my cardboard desk, something was being inculcated and habits of mind and heart were being formed.

It's November 20, 1957, a Wednesday. I would have been at home with my mother; it would have been cold outside, warm in our grey den, and doubtless I was in the early throes of pre-Thanksgiving holiday excitement. Garroway is walking back to his desk from another part of the studio and is met by *The Today Show*'s resident chimpanzee, who was dressed in a shirt, a vest, and—like Garroway himself—a bowtie. The existence of the chimp is perhaps the one fact most people recollect about the early *Today Show*, and it's cited as evidence that not everything was better then; that the Golden Age of Television was no less immune to gimmicks, vulgarity, and hokum as television is now. But wait.

As they reach they reach the desk, the chimp hands Garroway a bell, the tiny long handled kind you might use to summon the servants to the dining room in a stately home. Garroway says, "You've brought me a bell" as though he expects some sort of response but the chimp looks away. So Garroway continues, "I don't know, he's so whimsical these days. He's here and he's not here. He's there and he's not there. He brings a bell or he doesn't bring a bell."

Then he addresses the chimp again. "What's the immaculate significance of this bell?" he asks and waits. There's no response, and Garroway sits down and the chimp climbs up on the desk beside him, and picks up a book from it. "You won't talk, eh? I'll talk to you then. This is still National Children's Book Week, you know. And you're looking at one of the books I was going to read the poems from. Do you like poetry? Well, I'm glad you do. Because poetry is the great hope of man. Let me read you a couple of poems."

And he does. The chimp appears to be listening, or at least is not inattentive. He sits through one poem and another. This is live television, and while the chimp is "trained", he's shown himself to be intractable on other occasions. But what's fascinating is less the question of whether any of this could have been rehearsed than the rapport and relation between Garroway and the chimp. The inherent absurdity of the situation is a given, but so is a certain regard—what can only be called respect—in which Garroway holds the chimp and with him, the poetry, the audience, and the whole enterprise in which we are all involved together.

At age four I would, of course, have taken the whole thing at face value; and you might say that precisely the thing I was being taught by *The Today Show* was the virtue of taking things at face value. Our inclination today is, of course, very different, and we have our reasons; they are reasons that, in fact, predate *The Today Show*, modern reasons born at the beginning of the last century that still fiercely ramify, echo, and metamorphose today. For us, Garroway and his program may epitomize the easy innocence and complacency of Eisenhower's America, the long heedless summer of a nation enjoying a respite from war and depression. But not of a few of us—even at the time— suspected that the innocence was insidious, a willfully unreflective high-mindedness beneath which hid injustices and hypocrisies America was unwilling to examine.

You can argue all of that, and I might add that Garroway's most outrageous remark was "poetry is the great hope of man" (and not merely because it was made to a chimpanzee): not because it isn't true, but because we wish it were true and feel we know otherwise. Certainly I, as I sat behind my cardboard box (had it previously contained a case of Dreft or Crisco or Birds-Eye Lima Beans?), would have believed it. I would have believed it because a grown-up with a deep and tender voice on television had said it, and because I was disposed believe it, having been disposed by my mother, the ballads and anthems on her Broadway cast albums, the implacably serene and long-suffering nuns, the NBC Television Network and the grey den to be so disposed.

These things are relative—right after the poetry segment that morning in 1957 there was a program promo for a backward look at "the gaiety and charm of America's innocent years" —as, by the fact and force of time, they must be. Pretty much everything we say and feel today can be made to seem platitudinous and self-regarding tomorrow, and our best intentions and beliefs may someday sound like smug, self-deluding uplift. Perhaps the worst that can be said about the sensibility with which I was being inculcated was that it was sentimental. I could not, of

course, have told you then what "sentimental" meant:
whether it was a thing, a color, a sound, or some
juxtaposition of all these; not precisely the chalky cold air
outside with the first snowflakes swarming through it nor
the radiator-heated air inside, the man with the bowtie and
spectacles on the gray TV screen saying something
"whimsical" (the term's "immaculate significance" was
beyond me), nor the creak of the paint roller against the
wall, but my sense of being placed in just the way I was
amid all this, and it being safe, warm, and right. I did
know—my mother had told me—that Garroway's theme
song, which he had brought with him from his radio days in
Chicago, was "Sentimental Journey".

I would not have understood sentimental to mean
mawkish, nostalgic, or tending to believe what experience
and history gainsays—the complex of attitudes Hemingway
(himself then a little sentimental about the "Papa" persona
he had made for himself in the 1930s) deconstructed with
the line "Isn't it pretty to think so?" I hadn't heard it,
although the remark was as old as my mother. Nor would I
have understood sentimentality as a kind of warm tribute
the present pays to the past, having so little so past of my
own.

Oddly, I might have grasped the term more easily in its
older meaning—that of Laurence Sterne's *A Sentimental
Journey* (whence the title of Garroway's theme) of 1768—of
cultivated emotion, of training, harvesting, and enjoying the
higher sorts of feeling. There was, of course, a price to be
paid for such reflection. In his 1795 essay "On Naïve and
Sentimental Poetry" Friedrich von Schiller contrasted the
unselfconscious, "naïve" artist of a prior age with his
contemporary "sentimental" counterpart whose awareness
of his own feelings and thoughts, of his role as artist, and of
his location in history have become a kind of trap. By 1869,
in Flaubert's novel *Sentimental Education*, the sentimentalist

hero is a would-be writer who means to write a great novel but can't get started; who avoids or distracts himself from work by pursuing an impossible love-affair, while around him great events transpire to which he, in his narcissism, is oblivious. We are by this point very close to the notion of the sentimental as self-indulgent wallow; to a legion of barroom bores who announce, "I'm feeling a little sentimental tonight".

Perhaps Garroway's art was, by Schiller's definition, not sentimental but naïve, engaging directly with the world without the buffers of interpretation or self-regard. Certainly, it did not seem self-conscious, but neither did it trade exclusively in whimsy, in what we might today tend to regard as naive: how could it, with the shadow of World War II just behind it and the hydrogen bomb looming just ahead, not some years from now but in Frank Blair's next news report?

Could that have been lost on me? I do know I was a connoisseur of a certain kind of terror induced by Disney's versions of "Snow White", "Bambi", and "Sleeping Beauty" and *Grimm's Fairy Tales*, but its height was achieved in Prokofiev's *Peter and the Wolf*, as recorded and narrated by Arthur Godfrey. Godfrey, like Garroway, was mellow of voice and persona, albeit with a hint of a rasp, a tinge of smoke and perhaps rust. Where there was a suggestion of loss or regret in Garroway (he was said to have a drinking problem prompted by grief), there was a note of impatience or irritation in Godfrey (he was known to have a temper), and perhaps I detected in it some menace or threat that lent itself well to the material.

Peter, you probably know, is a lively, curious, and well-meaning boy being raised in the Russian taiga by a choleric grandfather. Between their house and the dark forest there's a meadow, reached through a gate, with a pond around which Peter's animal friends—a duck, a bird, and a cat—congregate. Peter's grandfather's role consists entirely of warning Peter of the dark and irreparable things that will happen if he passes beyond the gate, chiefly that he will be eaten by a large and terrible wolf. Thus are the all

"I've been saying it for 6 years now—and I'll say it again...much milder Chesterfield is best for me."

ingredients and conditions of juvenile tragedy set in place: there is a grumpy, admonishing adult, friends and cohorts whose qualities can be comprehended only by children, a dark and dangerous locale, a beast, and a hero whose Aristotelian flaw is to be a boy not so very different from you. But because this is a juvenile tragedy—which is to say a comedy that is scary until almost the very end—the tragic fate will be visited on the skeptical adult (he will be shown to be wrong, which is not such a bad thing); and the boy hero will, of course, save the day.

In Peter's case, Grandfather is right, at least for a while. There is a wolf and it comes into meadow and picks off several of Peter's animal friends, and it is gaining on Peter himself until Peter and his surviving friends turn the tables on the wolf, capturing him and shipping him off to the zoo in a triumphant march during which the local huntsmen fete Peter and Grandpa is made to eat crow.

This is bracing stuff for a four-year-old, and even after what must have been scores of playings, it never seemed to occur me that Peter wasn't in imminent danger. It is in the nature of children to be good conservators and recyclers of narrative, to be infinitely credulous in the face of a good story: it prolongs the pleasure, which in this is case is terror. It is better when the hero a child like you, and of course at a certain age every child—in stories, at least—is like you, but in this case I must have felt the child was especially like, well, me.

Tales of the vintage and provenance of *Peter and the Wolf* are redolent with the threat of abandonment or mischance in which every child is a potential foundling or orphan. Peter's own parents are glaringly absent; and to be down to one adult protector as he is with his grandfather is to be in some palpable sense one step closer to the wolf's gullet. My mother was not my grandfather nor was she grouchy, but our situation seemed to me more similar to Peter's than most children's. We did not live on the edge of the forest, but on a block of small mock-Tudor late 1940s houses. I

was not an only child, but I had a sister who had seen a
stranger's hand—she swore she had—appear in her room
through a slice in the screen on her window. Nor was the
wolf at the gate or at our door. But it was—I swore it was;
I knew it to be so—behind the furnace in the basement.

So *Peter and the Wolf* was not merely a story but my life
reflected, reconstituted, and brought back to life again on a
record. And that is before even considering the fact of the
music, which takes the story—the motifs and events that
line up to make a narrative—and transmutes it into
something that was large and deep enough to take total
possession of me. Some of this is a matter of extending and
rounding out what is already implicit: that Peter, for
example, is impetuous goes almost without saying. But the
skipping lilt of the violins in his theme don't just confirm
but substantiate this in an almost literal sense; renders it
solid.

Similarly, we don't need to be told that the wolf is dark
and menacing, but just how dark and menacing we don't
appreciate until we hear the hulking French horn that
represents him lurking at the edge of the forest. And while
the two themes and the two characters obviously are in
opposition and contrast to one another and are headed
towards some kind of collision, they are also in
counterpoint: they are composed from the same
materials—notes, keys, and motifs—arranged in different
ways, but in symmetrical relation to one another.

There is much more of this kind of thing, and I
probably grasp it less well to day than I did then: we know
from the musical form of their themes that the bird is
dutiful but a hysteric, that the cat is a bit shiftless, and that
the duck is melancholic—accustomed to and designed for
loss—and so we know well before it happens that he is
destined to be sacrificed to the wolf. For me, the most
satisfying moment in *Peter and the Wolf* is also the most

disconcerting: hearing the muted oboe of the duck's theme that we are told is issuing from the wolf's stomach. To a child's mode of thinking, of course the duck is still alive in there, and will be until someone gets him out. But there's no suggestion in either Godfrey's narration or in the music that this is ever going to happen.

It's here, I think, that for all conventionality of its constituent parts that *Peter and the Wolf* evades sentimentality in its hackneyed sense and moves beyond to something altogether larger. The pathos is here—we're meant to feel for the duck, even to cry for him—but we're not allowed to leave it at that. In addition, we're asked to do some imaginative labor: to consider what it's like to be trapped (for all time perhaps) in the wolf's stomach when you are a melancholy duck; moreover, to consider what it feels like to be fated to have this happen to you, both on the grounds of chance and because something in you—in your character—has caused this to happen. In other words, we've been asked to contemplate the tragic and to do so by means of the sentimental in its oldest, deepest sense: to feel our way into lives of others, into their unique, private, and necessary subjectivities; the prison of one or another wolf's stomach.

I don't claim to have understood this at the age of four or five. But I surely grasped it, if only in assenting so heartily to being grasped by *it*, repeatedly, almost, you might say, to the point of exhaustion. We had art around us, my mother and sister and me, in the newly painted grey den and in Dave Garroway, but here I was in the presence of art at full tilt: not just of a piece with the world, reflecting and refracting it, with luck explaining and enriching it, but here exceeding it in density and amplitude, distilled down to one amber bittersweet drop.

I think it was at this time that I began to prefer art to what most people would call life; to favor reading and listening to music and watching the television over games, sports, or playing with other children. I had friends of course, but what were they compared to the cat, the bird, and the duck? We had fun; we even had what would have called adventures (that large and frightening dog was still around the neighborhood; he chased us; he became, for a breathless instant, the wolf); but we scarcely had themes by Prokofiev, scored for an orchestra, to identify and deepen our characters; nor did we have lyricists like Hammerstein or Comden and Green to give us words to sing, to explain how we felt.

But isn't art necessarily artificial, and so isn't this a little sad, this child for whom reality is a disappointment, who takes solace in artifice, in invention and the necessarily false? Certainly, I was a little lonely and perhaps even a little bored: every little mock-Tudor house on our little block had a father, just as it had a Ford or Chevrolet sedan and two to four children, so my own father's absence loomed large and made the facts of our situation less palatable than the products of my own and others imaginations. So, yes, I was inclined to make the most of whatever befell me, to extract the maximum amount of excitement and, yes, drama from daily life; to try to turn it into something closer to art.

I would have known that this could be done. My mother's Broadway cast albums did it, sometimes profoundly. Rodgers and Hammerstein's *Carousel* spun literal corn ("A Real Nice Clambake") into tragedy ("Soliloquy") and then resignation or perhaps even redemption ("You'll Never Walk Alone", which admittedly evades corn by just a whisker). It also suggested that fathers who disappear and die might nevertheless want to make their presence felt. In this there seemed be hope for boys like me who otherwise might tend to be at once too trusting of some men (men with deep and tender voices on the radio and TV) and overly suspicious of others (practically every one I knew excepting one uncle). This was art I could use.

I was therefore in pursuit by the age of five of what I would learn at age twenty to call the transcendent. Art transcended life. What, then, transcended art? Perhaps a kind of meta-art, something like Wagner's notion of the *gesamtkunstwerk*, opera as total artwork. I found mine, at least for that passage of my life, on NBC on Christmas Eve.

I might almost say I gestated along with Menotti's *Amahl and the Night Visitors*. I was conceived the summer it was composed and I suppose my brain was pretty well formed in my mother's womb by the time of its premiere in December 1951. It was performed on NBC almost every Christmas thereafter through the early sixties. I suppose the first time I would have watched it with any comprehension was around the time my mother painted the den; and it seems to me now to be of a piece with the other things that were forming me at that time.

It was high art by the standards of television, broadcast on *The Hallmark Hall of Fame*, the home of prestige productions of Shakespeare, Ibsen, and Shaw. That these should be sponsored by the arch-purveyor of cheap, canned sentiment, a greeting card company, must have been an irony lost at the time on every one, or—as with Garroway, poetry, and the chimp—on no one, entailing an understanding of the relation between art and sentiment for which we have lost the knack; that and the notion of the middlebrow, of communicating the importance of high art to the masses together with judiciously chosen samples of it.

What was not lost on me surely was that Amahl was another impetuous boy—handicapped but all the more plucky for it—being raised by one adult in an out of the way place. That adult, like the grandfather in Peter, is weary and suspicious of the boy's impetuousness, which in this case takes the form of a propensity for fanciful exaggeration. As in Peter, the adult is shown up: Amahl hasn't cried wolf; in fact, the gravity and magnificence of what he has stumbled upon is lost on him until the end of the story. Nor does he save the day. Rather, everything and everyone including Amahl is saved by the extraordinary nature of what he's discovered and forced the adults around him to comprehend.

The comparisons of course only go so far, and in my case the differences are just as striking. The adults, for one, are Amahl's mother and her unexpected guests, the magi on their way to Bethlehem. Amahl's mother, for all her hard-headedness, is a kind of saint, impoverished, abandoned or widowed, and struggling to raise her crippled son. My mother and I were not impoverished and she and my father had had a relatively amicable divorce. But I knew the dynamic of the relation between mother and son in such situations, the striking oddness of it in a world of perfectly rounded nuclear families, as well as the isolation it engendered. But I also knew that certain camaraderie it fostered; that, and a faintly subversive humor in the face of all those other households that were ordinary and normal while ours, abnormal, was in my imagination's happier moments special in its oddness, flamboyant even in its grey den.

Neither, of course, was I handicapped or crippled. But at that time, handicaps had a perhaps extraordinary resonance. The Roosevelt years were still fresh in people's minds, polio outbreaks continued through the decade, and the March of Dimes was perhaps the country's most prominent charity. Crutches, wheelchairs, and iron lungs were part of the landscape. My own father, I dimly knew as I watched Amahl, was being tended in his own iron lung and cripple's bed by his new wife back in Boston.

The climax of Amahl, of course, is and must be the healing of Amahl's handicap, its miraculous and unwarranted removal after Amahl's mother, in her desperation, tries to steal the Magi's gold and Amahl defends and protects her from the consequences of her crime. The magi are compelled to realize that Amahl and his mother need their gold more than the child whose star they are following. Then comes the miracle. Amahl asks his mother for permission to go with the magi to give thanks to the newborn king who is his benefactor. His mother agrees (provided he dresses warmly). The mother has been forgiven, she and Amahl are no longer poor, and Amahl himself is healed and in some sense a man, but will, of course, return to her.

I loved this as much as I was moved by it. I could not enjoy it again and again as I could Peter—it was only broadcast once a year—but I doubt I would have wanted to.

It was, together with Prokofiev's duck, my first experience with art that dealt in pity, with "the tears of things", and it must have been a bit wrenching, this encounter with the tragic; or, in this case with tragedy redeemed, operating under the auspices of the Christian God rather than Aristotle's. It was still sad, but the sadness was tempered by the possibility of mercy and even joy, or at least forbearance. Nor did it imply that character—say, a character like mine; impetuous, but also lonely and sometimes simply bad—was necessarily destiny. Here art not only magnified and exceeded life but in some way promised to redeem it.

Certainly Amahl was a sentimental piece, but given my age and my culture with its benign view of the purposes and effects of art, I simply felt my way inside his skin and that of his mother like anyone in the audience. This, too, would have been in the mode of the sentimental in its original form. I would have felt sorrow and pity for them and this would have been regarded as a good thing for me. What's more, I would have thought it was good for them in some way, as though they might draw strength from the intensity of my feelings; as though my beliefs about them were not simply a sort of fanciful regard, but a kind of love.

Perhaps this is not so very different from rooting for the hero and hissing the villain, and as an approach to life or art, it begs some significant questions. How, for example, do we inhabit the skins and sentimentally engage with alien or less than sympathetic characters or situations? Not to mention that today, imaginative sympathy of the kind I was exercising is a little suspect. It seems to appropriate and distort the lives of the real-world poor, handicapped, and alien, to subject them for our own selfish purposes to smug high-mindedness. We seem confused, perhaps rightly so, about the distinctions among identifying and sympathizing and sentimentalizing, all of which seem to occur in one way or another at the expense of the objects of our curiosity and feeling.

Yet to enjoy, be moved by and find instructive Peter or Amahl is not to say that we approve of boys being crippled or poor or put in the path of dangerous predators; nor is it to feel superior to them nor to have our prejudices confirmed. Anyway, you could not have told me I didn't mean well by Peter and the duck or Amahl and his mother. And it went without saying that they did me good, that I was in a real way enlarged by them. I was able to picture not just people and lives beyond the ambit of our house and town but to see and, however briefly, grasp the ineffably beautiful, the numinous and the miraculous. Feeling my way into—sentimentalizing—Amahl, I might have thought that this might have been my life; that I might be capable of acting in some broader compass; that maybe something like this—something miraculous and lovely—could happen to me, something I had never imagined before. Perhaps this gift, this redemption, for lack of a better word, that *Amahl and the Night Visitors* seemed to promise was the way out of the wolf's stomach.

That took me as far as art could then take me then. What we require and what we can comprehend and make use of changes, of course. Sometimes we need the magi or Peter's duck, and sometimes Faust or Fra Angelico's Angel of the Annunciation or George Eliot's Dorthea Brooke or Dostoevsky's Grand Inquisitor and sometimes we merely need Garroway and Kokomo the chimp. But by then, pretty much by the time that the den was completely painted, I knew something about art and its limits. Art transcended and in some way redeemed life. Yet there was a limit that you might prod and test, but perhaps never surpass: the thing or being that might transcend art, the transcendent itself. That, of course, was an idea, an abstraction (what I would later learn from Kant is called a category), and I was stuck among things, in the world. Things incorporated the limit of art and the world and of myself, but that did not seem so very bad to me then.

I was already acquainted with the tragic and with the hope of enduring or even overcoming it, but I didn't feel it had ever visited us. The small wounds I had experienced had hurt and they ached a little—sometimes more often than not—but they'd never attained the critical mass of tragedy or terror. I suffered them quietly as I might suffer a lonely night in my little bed or a day too cold to play outside. When I was being very good, I imagined I suffered them as the nuns or Amahl's mother or God's mother suffered; perhaps even as my own mother suffered—though I could not sentimentalize her yet, for I needed her to be a God.

This, too, and perhaps mainly, is why I needed art: not to escape the darkness, the cold, the necessity of the wolf's belly, but to transmute it. Even then, I must have begun to understand it wasn't a cure or even much of a distraction. Art invoked suffering as memory invokes the past, and there are tears and pain in that. Perhaps it only really frames the misery or pretties it up so that we can swallow it before it swallows us. Or at best transforms incoherence, chaos, and privation into the world of things, of being, where we live, and must live with it, in patterns we can apprehend a little, if not comprehend.

For example, I see—I feel—some meaning in the fact that Dave Garroway, Arthur Godfrey, and Chet Allen, the original Amahl, all died within a year of each other, in 1982 and '83. Garroway committed suicide. He had just appeared on the thirtieth anniversary celebration of *The Today Show*, from which he had been fired in 1961. Godfrey had managed to stay on the air until the early seventies, but thereafter could find no more work: he had made, it was said, too many enemies. He died from lung cancer and emphysema, from the cigarettes that had given him his distinctive voice, that he hawked on the air with such effectiveness.

Chet Allen was offered a three-picture movie contract on account of his performance in Amahl, but only made one film, *Meet Me at the Fair* with Dan Dailey and Diana Lynn in 1952. He ended up back in Columbus, Ohio, in whose boys choir Menotti had found him. He was admitted to and released from a series of mental hospitals, and as an adult worked for ten years as a stock boy in a Columbus store. At age 44, he managed to save up a large supply of his antidepressant medication and killed himself. Menotti had once looked him up in Columbus. He hadn't ever gotten over being Amahl, the composer thought; "Allen needed more care and attention than anyone could give him".

But what does this mean? Into what can it be shaped? That ambition and celebrity are dangerous? We knew that, I suppose. Perhaps it is art that is dangerous and some profound way—because it is created, made-up, imagined—false. Godfrey's warm voice made his heart bitter. Poetry was not the great hope of man, not for Garroway, who abandoned all hope. Art could not heal Chet Allen, nor, apparently, could the child, king, and god whom Amahl went to thank for the miracle save him.

Art is not, we must believe, the answer. It will not redeem us. But perhaps it is the only thing that deliberately points us in the direction of hoping otherwise—of living in the world of things and imagining more things, of entering into them and learning from them and loving them; of then imagining that that feeling, and not the pain, was at the heart of things. Wouldn't it be pretty to think so?

Maybe I needed more and better imagination, more, yes, sentimentality, not less. And that in spite of the self-consciousness it entails, which as, Schiller saw, is kind of curse, an expulsion from the Eden of the naïve. For me,

though, it was already too late to go back, even at age four:
I had already seen things—suffering, betrayal, and loss—
from which I could never again avert my eyes. But maybe
sentimentality, far from being an evasion of death and
sorrow, is the vehicle by which we accommodate and
acknowledge tragedy in our lives. At any rate, I knew what
I needed—perhaps, to keep me from needing more care
and attention than anyone could give me.

By the time I was five, I was pretty sure of it. I was
playing at my cousins' house one day, the house of my
paternal aunt and her minister husband. I did not go there
often. There was, understandably, a certain tension
between my father's family and my mother. They blamed
her, maybe with reason, for the divorce, and implicitly, for
his having moved back east, to Boston, where there was

polio, from which he was now apparently dying. His family, and particularly my aunt, were also devout Calvinists for whom smoking and drinking were anathema. They would have regarded Arthur Godfrey pitching Chesterfields as an invitation to perdition, and perhaps for Godfrey, they were more right than they knew.

But that day, there was music on the record player, not the kind of music we played at our house, but conventional children's music: nursery rhymes or "Tubby the Tuba" or something along those lines. I asked my aunt if perhaps they had something else. Something "classical". Like what, she asked? Well, I explained, maybe something like *South Pacific* or *Carrousel* or *On the Town*.

My aunt explained that what I had in mind wasn't really classical music, and that in any case, they didn't have anything like that at their house. I was impetuous enough that I may have allowed that this was too bad for them. Anyway, I was given to understand that I was mistaken about the music. That I already knew something about real classical music from Sister Anne and the nuns proved nothing: in my aunt's eyes, the Roman church, with its pathos and arty ceremony and fondness for suffering bodies, was of a piece with Broadway. I knew I was meant to feel at least a little silly and perhaps somewhat shameful for having thought otherwise.

For all I knew, the matter ended there, but apparently telephone calls were made to various relations and eventually to my mother. My aunt was not simply chagrined but appalled that my mother had inculcated in me a taste for such music. It was utterly inappropriate for a child, still less for a boy who now lacked firm masculine guidance. It was superficial, sophisticated, and sentimental music composed, for all she knew, by alcoholics and homosexuals. On this last matter she was probably right, but at our house quite a few of my mother's friends were one or the other or both of these. In fact, she was not far away from marrying one of them.

It took my aunt, so my mother told me later, a while to find the exact word to describe the character of this milieu into which she accused my mother of acculturating and educating me. My mother would have liked to say that my aunt sputtered, but in truth my aunt was neither stupid nor a stock old biddy: by the standards of that time and place, she fairly normal in her tastes and beliefs, and it was my mother who was odd.

My aunt settled on the word "worldly". That was the nature of the things that I was being formed by, and I was in danger of it becoming my nature. Certainly it was true that I had already come to admire and even love certain things, and these things were very much of the world rather than of the spirit, by which I suppose my aunt would have meant the eternal, the true, and the good as summed up in God. And as against the superficial, the false, and the malign, the spirit had a lot to recommend it.

Admittedly, I didn't know much about the spiritual or about God. My mother was a lapsed Episcopalian and we sporadically attended a Unitarian church where I may have heard that Jesus was a great teacher, on a par, I would have guessed, with NBC's Mr. Wizard. Other than that, I knew the ideal and the spiritual by way of the world: by way of Garroway's alchemizing of grief and wonder into whimsy and tenderness; or of the bravery, pity, and sublime terror I found in *Peter and the Wolf*; or of the quotidian heartache and joy transfigured by music on my mother's Broadway albums. Even my closest encounters with the notion of God were indirect. Amahl has its miracle, but God and Jesus (identified only as "the child") are at some considerable remove, at the end of a journey we do not witness. And while the nursery school I attended with saturated with religion—with statues and crucifixes and rustling habits and clicking beads—I don't recall anything like proselytizing or even prayer taking place. Perhaps the presence of God went without saying. He was the boss, the employer, of these nuns. He was an unseen presence in the office upstairs, but everything that went on here was his business.

I think I would have found the idea that the world and the spirit were in opposition a little confusing. What little I knew of the spirit I knew through the world; and pushed a little further I might have felt that while the idea of a god didn't compel you to imagine the world, the fact of there being a world lead almost inexorably to the idea of it having an author; a creator or artist like Prokofiev or Menotti or Bernstein to set it in motion, on a somewhat larger scale.

In a sense, however, my aunt may have been on to something, although perhaps not what she intended. Maybe she was right to be wary of worldly sentiments, be it the self-conscious paralysis of the frustrated novelist or the cheap analgesic of misty-eyed nostalgia. And, yes, sometimes they end up—not necessarily, but at least contingently—forming the life of a Chet Allen. But these are afflictions of the spirit, aren't they? They come of self-knowledge. My aunt might have called it original sin. I would now call it the spirit—or at least the mind—blinded and dazzled by its own brilliance and unmoored from the world of things; a self cut loose from its own createdness, from the world, and from suffering and joy and therefore real transcendence, which is found not in ideas but in things.

So, yes, I was worldly. I loved the world, and I had learned to love it by way of art, of consciously created things. Before I came to know it through them, I was mostly afraid of it. But it taught me to love, and what it taught me to love most of all was itself and therefore whomever or whatever had made it. I wasn't going to be saved by my aunt's lights, but maybe I was going to be saved by the world. Loving it, I might even imagine that the world—or someone or something in it—might love me. I'd felt my way into it, naively, sentimentally, and now I was worldly.

2.

LIFE WITH FATHER

Bob was one of my mother's boy friends. He was not my favorite but he was the one she married. There was, for example, Joe, who always brought an ice cream roll for my sister and me; Irving, whose house had a pond we could skate on in winter; and Henry, who was a photographer and had a kind of glamour on that account. By contrast, Bob did not make much of an impression on me until I was five years old when he and my mother announced they were going to marry.

What my mother's boyfriends almost all had in common was that they were gay. In the case of Joe, Irving, and Henry, at some point it became "common knowledge". As for Bob, he told me himself. That, of course, was later. So in most of what follows, the facts—what I knew when I was five and what I knew when I was, say, twenty-five, and what I've discovered in the last few years—occur on parallel levels that don't fully overlap, until just now.

They're all true, these facts: the revelation of one doesn't falsify another, or even necessarily color it or call for its re-evaluation. If this were a drama, we might see ironies unfolding, but as it stands I see only varieties of innocence, of taking things at face value as they change and weather with time. They changed me—they still are changing me, I suppose—though scarcely in ways anyone might have imagined. And of course everything might have been otherwise.

Bob's family owned a large and well thought-of chain of flower stores and greenhouses, and Bob, who had a degree in horticulture, oversaw several of these. In addition to arranging flowers, he liked interior design and figure skating. He loved society gossip and had a high, tittering, screeching laugh. At some point in their courtship he advised my mother that he was "well hung", which, as she pointed out many years later, was, however well meant, perhaps not the most romantic thing to say to a girl.

Now perhaps you, the reader, are already asking how my mother could possibly *not* know what sort of man she was involved with. Were this a novel, you would be having trouble finding the characters "believable".

Let me try again in terms a fictionalist might use. What did these characters believe? What was at stake for them? What did they *want*? Bob surely wanted position and status, and there simply wasn't much of either attached to the role of "confirmed bachelor" for the son of second-generation Swedish immigrants, no matter how successful. As for "coming out", the concept didn't even exist: not in Minnesota, not in 1957

Bob's first wife—he'd tried before, he was persistent, not to say ambitious—was the heiress to a brewing fortune. At the greenhouse, the employees called her "the duchess". The marriage was childless and broke up after perhaps two years, eighteen months or so before Bob set his sights on my mother. Socially, she wasn't in the duchess's league: she wasn't rich, and while she was from a pedigreed "old St. Paul" family, they were no longer in the top tier.

But she would do. For one thing, she was fun. She liked to go out and socialize and drink. She knew people—the kind of people Bob wanted to meet—and she had, by St. Paul standards, a sense of style. He'd seen the grey den, the blonde furniture, and her chic short Italian haircut. He liked what he saw—the surfaces—and so he liked her, after his fashion. Bob was, as my mother would later say, "deeply superficial".

She liked him in the same way. He was lively. He liked to work around the house and in the garden. He was eager, almost hungry, to attach himself to her family, to her whole milieu. More seriously for her, the position of single mother was no more tenable at that time and place than was "confirmed bachelor". It was expected—it went without saying—that she would remarry. The most compelling imperative of all was to provide a father for her children and, in particular, "masculine influence" for her son—for me.

According to the parenting experts of the time, the need for "masculine influence" was no mere matter of what we now call "role models". Psychology was at the apex of its prestige as a science, and the literature, the scientific laws, stated that a boy needed a father for the obvious reasons—the inculcation of masculine culture and pursuits like sports, hunting, and camping—but more crucially as a necessary counterbalance to his mother. Mothers were essential to their sons in their own way, but left to their own subconscious devices, absent a countervailing man within the family drama, they were as pernicious as communist sleeper agents. Simply put, single mothers (especially ones with domineering, strong, or flamboyant personalities) caused homosexual pathology in their sons.

I can't say exactly how much this weighed on my mother or if it was on her mind when she accepted Bob's proposal. It didn't need to be: it was in the water like fluoride, in the air like fallout. My mother had majored in psychology in college. She knew the science. On the other hand, I can't recall my mother ever in her life saying a derogatory word about a gay or lesbian person or about homosexuality in general. But you didn't toy with pathology. You didn't put your son in its path.

So Bob and my mother—absurdly, wrongly, if for apparently right reasons—needed each other. They married in a small ceremony conducted by a Unitarian minister in my grandparent's living room. One didn't make a display of second marriages. While the rite transpired I was minded by a babysitter in an adjacent room for fear that in a burst of rambunction I might disrupt the solemnities. I resented this, but I also can't say that I might not have been tempted to burst into, say, "The Oldest Established Floating Crap Game in New York" from *Guys and Dolls* during the blessing or the vows.

And what did I need? Transcendence, I think, although this was not a word I would learn until ten years later, under the tutelage of another masculine influence. Of course, I wanted and needed what every child does: security, affection, and the freedom to grow in accord with my own inner inclinations. But I also sought some deeper, closer embodiment of the way music, images, and stories made me *feel*; a tactile sense of their origin—their creator or, perhaps, father—whose presence it seemed to me must somehow be attained and apprehended.

I didn't know the word for it, but I knew what I was after. I sought it by means of beauty, love, and faith. I didn't understand those things as concepts either, but whenever I happened on them I knew them and slipped into them as easily as a pair of my black high-top sneakers. When I was happy and unafraid, the days ahead of me seemed numberless, the spaces I might inhabit illimitable. I had a kind of faith by default and I existed leaning into what seemed the head wind of eternity. I was forever in mid-leap—in the gap between being poised to jump and landing—throwing myself into the world. It did not occur to me to know as adults do that the only guaranteed encounter with eternity we have is in death. I rode around—as parents then allowed children to do—standing heedlessly on the front seat of the car, taking it all in as though I were king.

After the honeymoon—Bob and my mother went to the Virgin Islands while my sister and I stayed with that same babysitter—we moved to a new house Bob had bought in another Minnesota city. It was capacious compared to our old mock Tudor and had a large yard and was near the school where I would begin kindergarten. I quickly saw that my new life could be congenial. I made friends in the neighborhood, built a succession of forts and hideouts in the alleys and parks nearby, and learned to ride a two-wheeler. This last took some doing: on the slope outside our house, I kept crashing headlong into trees and parked cars. My nose flared blood; my knees were abraded to the consistency of hamburger.

But while I was warming to some of these masculine (or at least boyish) pursuits, some of my other interests became cause for concern. In kindergarten, I conceived a fascination for washing machines, detergents, and dryers. I collected empty miniature boxes of soap from a local launderette and haunted our basement laundry room, paying obeisance to the Maytags. At some point I discovered (perhaps through an ad on Saturday morning TV) the existence of a child-scaled toy washing machine and I announced that for my next birthday this was my heart's desire.

I was an acquisitive and fanciful kid, full of wishes and requests, and in the normal course of things these were granted, refused, or shrugged off without much ceremony, by one parent or the other. But this occasion prompted a full-scale family Summit Meeting (held, or so I want to remember it, in my very sanctum sanctorum, the laundry room) with both my mother and Bob. They stood together and tried to persuade me that I didn't really want *this* particular toy, and when I proved unmovable, explained that although I might think I wanted it, this was not a boy's toy, but a toy for a girl. Surely I didn't want a girl's toy?

But I did. I didn't care. But I should care, Bob and my mother said more darkly. It was *odd* for a boy to own such a toy. People would think I was odd. Other boys would think

I was odd. I don't know why this didn't persuade me. I must have been impassioned or obsessed. I might have replied that I was only going to use the washing machine in the privacy of our basement; that no one would know.

Here the mood—and it is the mood rather than the words spoken that I recall so precisely—became grave. I was given to understand that having the toy washer was not merely silly or socially awkward but dangerous: that having it could harm me; that I could catch something from it that would make me less of a boy, a sick boy.

I knew about being a sissy. I wasn't one—not yet. But this unspecified infection was worse than that. Bob and my mother didn't give it a name or describe the symptoms. They merely impressed upon me that it was very, very serious. I knew the etiology—toy washing machines—and the disease's progress—sissification leading to debilitation and misery—but no more. How much simpler if Bob had simply said, "It will make you into someone like *me*. And despite appearances, I am ashamed and unhappy."

But by that time I liked Bob. We had worked together in the backyard. He had taught me to ride my bike. He had a given me a silly nickname. I liked him and I wouldn't have minded being like him one bit. And we were happy, all of us, and no one was ashamed of anything.

As it turned out, I got the toy washing machine. It was my first guilty pleasure. It sat in the basement next to the big, grown-up Maytags, and I lost interest in it after perhaps a month. Of course, a month is a very long time when you are five-going-on-six, but that was the end of my interest in gender-inappropriate toys. That's not to say I didn't remain a little "odd". I continued to have a fascination with basements, boxes and containers, and underground passages and chambers, with caves and snow forts and hollow trees. They made a kind of underground world and perhaps, in that, I knew Bob better than I might have imagined.

J.C. and Robert - Winter 1958

Bob, meanwhile, was beginning to immerse me in "masculine influence" and I was glorying in it. He bought a motorboat and I got a sailor hat and played the first mate. We went hunting, tramping through gelid cornfields searching for pheasant. And we not only went camping, but went camping with a whole Boy Scout troop of which Bob was the scoutmaster. (Don't laugh. Or wince. Of course he was a scoutmaster, just as he was a florist and a member of the Jaycees and drove a Ford Country Squire station wagon.). It was like having the ultimate dad and a dozen big brothers.

We went on fabulous vacations to San Francisco, Disneyland, and Aspen. At home, Bob built us a new house closer to the countryside and bought a jazzy new black Oldsmobile convertible with red upholstery. Best of all, Bob had a dog—a cocker spaniel—and it became my dog. We tramped all over the woods and fields around our new house. We found, if not a cave, at least a hollow lined with

rock, a sort of tiny black walled canyon in which the dog
and I could hide.

That's not to say I was a loner. I had three or four close
friends. We built forts and tree houses and they knew my
secret places. We had cap guns and rifles and canteens and
cowboy boots. My friends came over to our house on
Saturday mornings to watch TV with me. The day-maid
Bob had hired would make us all pancakes and we'd eat
them in front of *Sky King* and *Yogi Bear*.

My mother and Bob had more friends than me, many
more. In addition to tracking down and attaching
themselves to the city's leading Episcopalians and Harvard
graduates, Bob and my mother were almost lousy with

doctors, heart surgeons, and celebrity specialists. The city was the home of a famous clinic, and perhaps Bob's most prized social connection was to the younger generation of the clinic's founders, the Mayos, together with access to their estate, Mayowood.

Bob owed that social success to my mother, and he was frank about it. My mother was gracious and charming and fun; she seemed indifferent to people's position, and I think she largely was. Bob, on the other hand, perhaps less frankly, wanted to drop their names, drink and gossip in their swell homes and country clubs, and acquire them as customers. They weren't in any sense strictly my mother's friends, but in the siege of Mayowood it was my mother who'd conquered.

There was another couple, however, which Bob had discovered himself, and they were perhaps my mother and Bob's most frequent companions. Their names were Ted and Janet and what I chiefly recall about them is that they were young (younger than Bob, who was several years younger than my mother) and attractive. Ted was as fit and handsome as an astronaut and Janet was pretty and blonde in Scandinavian/Californian mode, which at that time was the gold standard of American beauty.

I don't know—I'm sure I never knew—much more about them. Whatever Ted did—he wasn't a doctor—it was not consequential enough to mention, nor were the forebears or provenance of either him or Janet. But they had an impact on us. Bob began hunting when they came along, and the four of them shot skeet from our backyard. I can recall any number of trudges through the cornfields in late autumn with Bob and Ted in the vanguard with their shotguns, myself just behind in a state of high excitement, and my mother and Janet resignedly and dutifully bringing up the rear.

I know that neither Janet nor my mother liked the hunting or most of Bob and Ted's other masculine pastimes, but they didn't commiserate; and it seemed clear to me that was because they didn't like each other either. On the subject of Janet, my mother's customary graciousness gave way to something close to snobbery. What Janet made of my mother, I don't know, but there were no warm feelings. They both knew, I suppose, what was up.

I can recall my mother complaining and rolling her eyes about having to socialize with Ted and Janet, and I know I heard her and Bob fight about having to see them again.

She'd rather have gone to Mayowood. I didn't know the impetus or context of these conflicts. In any case, they would soon be fighting about many things.

Later, when I was a teenager, my mother was frank in saying that she assumed Bob and Ted had been having an affair. Two decades later, I was able to ask Bob about it. He was uncharacteristically cagey. You might think he was reluctant to confess he had cheated on my mother, but today I'm more inclined to think he had gotten nowhere with Ted despite all his eager, almost fawning efforts. Ted, I think, had rejected him; had broken his heart—such a heart as he had.

I make the qualification knowing that, however much I liked him, Bob was accustomed to and practiced in cruelty. His parents were nasty and cold, and there was mutual contempt between him and his only sibling, an older brother named Skip. When matters began to escalate between Bob and my mother—the staggering and cursing and wailing that woke me and my sister from our sleep at one in the morning—the rancor was both bitter and gleeful. I recall a night when my mother took a hammer and pounded for five minutes on the master bedroom door behind which Bob had locked himself. When the door finally sprang open, Bob was nowhere to be found. He'd lowered himself out a window and let himself back into the lower level of the house where I discovered him lying on the upper mattress of my bunk bed, smirking.

By this time I was eight years old, going into the third grade. I had, if not sophistication, a certain satiric take on the world and its deceptions and pretensions, especially regarding status seeking, political and corporate disingenuousness, and the idiocy of television and what *Mad* magazine, my bible, called "Madison Avenue ads".

So perhaps I was ready to adopt a cool, sidelong glance at what was to come, to be unsurprised at the tawdry and awful idiocy of grown-ups. One night that winter, Bob and my mother came home very late and very drunk from Mayowood. Bob or my mother—it was never clear who had been behind the wheel of the beautiful black convertible—drove into the garage and lowered the door with the automatic opener. Bob exited the car and went into the house through the connecting door, closing it after him. The engine was still running.

My mother was in the car, dozing or perhaps passed out from the night's drinking, her head on the dashboard. At some point she came to in the sealed garage, now clouded with fumes. Either she made her own way into the house—it's not clear from anything she and Bob ever said—or Bob returned and pulled her from the car.

The first I knew of any of this was the next morning, when I came upstairs and discovered a puppy, a basset

hound, in the house. Bob had gone out at dawn, found a
kennel, and brought him home. The rationale for this—the
shards of what had transpired the previous night—came out
slowly and disjointedly, but the crux was that my mother
had survived but our cocker spaniel, bedded down in his
basket in the garage for the night, had not.

I have to give Bob credit—it's no mean trick to gauge
the precisely needful thing a disastrous situation requires—
and I gave it to him then. I fell in love with the new dog,
and I named it Theodore. I don't think I gave the cocker
another thought. Perhaps I had learned a little about
callousness from Bob, or perhaps I was merely becoming
inured to the middling tragedy that visited itself upon
families like ours.

In retrospect, I see that Theodore was as much my
mother's dog as mine. He was a decorator dog, a
whimsical, Baroque creature designed to accent indoor
space rather than patrol the woods with an eight-year old.
But that was okay: I was a little Baroque myself. And I also
see that Bob was at that time "trying" with my mother in the
manner of couples at the marital precipice. We took one of
our trips to Chicago and did dinner and the show at the
Palmer House, where Joey Bishop came over to our table
and interviewed me and my sister as part of his act. My

mother, too, was "trying", but I am sure Bob wasn't having any fun.

We took our Chris-Craft out one weekend and camped on the deck. Theodore went overboard, got lost and drowned. Bob replaced him with an identical Basset named Theodora, who by temperament and sex was even more meant to be my mother's dog. It did no good. In April, Bob moved out, and in June he and my mother sat my sister and me down and announced they were divorcing.

I received the news somberly, with no great surprise or horror. This is how it goes, I thought to myself. There was a conference with the judge, a formality about which I'd been coached. He asked me if I wanted to stay with my mother or Bob. I said I wanted to stay with my mother, knowing full well I'd been having the time of my life for the previous four years with Bob. I exhaled, and my sense of the boundless, my faith in my run of infinite happiness, emptied out. But the masculine influence had taken: I'd acquired a sense of resignation in the face of duty—that, and the hardened-heart.

My mother, my sister, and I moved back up to St. Paul that summer. Two months later, Bob persuaded my mother to let me ride shotgun in one of the flower store's delivery trucks and come down to visit him for a day. I stood leaning forward on the floor in front of the passenger seat of the flat-fronted van, nose pressed against the glass of the windshield, as the highway ripped by just beneath my feet, as though the world were an aquarium. The truck dropped me at the flower store, and then Bob and I drove out to our old home. He'd already redecorated much of the house, reupholstering the den furniture in a masculine red plaid.

But the showpiece was the living room. Under joint administration with my mother, the walls had been painted a bland powder blue with couches and chairs to match, accented by pieces of Colonial-style furniture in oak and walnut. In the space of a few months, however, Bob had recovered the walls in yellow felt and brought in a pair of sumptuous divan sofas done up in yellow, white, and gold fabric with welting and cylindrical Roman-style pillows. I thought it looked swell. I wondered where Ted was.

I think I sensed Bob's audacity in this. I know now that Bob had done no more or less than import a taste of High Fag style to a medium-sized city in Minnesota. Within a year, he left for Los Angeles where that and so much of the rest of his life were not so strange and alien. In his wake, I later learned, there followed a fleet of collectors, bailiffs, and IRS agents as well his father, his brother, and my mother, who was in hot pursuit of her alimony payments. Our wonderful life—the house, the vacations, the boat and the convertible, the pedigreed dogs and the maid—had been conjured by Bob with funds embezzled from the flower business, unpaid debt, and tax dodges.

I didn't see him again for fourteen years. In the immediate wake of the divorce, however, there was a new home, a new school, and new classmates to adjust to. It did not go well. I was high-strung, attention seeking, and failing school. Within a year, I was in treatment with Dr. Wiener, a child-analyst (the significance of whose name—as phallic as it was Viennese—gave me endless mirth).

Dr. Wiener gave me tests and showed me Rorschachs and illustrations of adults glowering at one another. He asked me to make up stories about them and I obliged. But Dr. Wiener couldn't get anywhere with me. At last, he prescribed "masculine influence".

I was sent to an Episcopal Church boarding school in the south of the state, not too far from our old home with Bob. It was run on military lines and, with the exception of a housemother and a few day-teachers, the faculty was entirely male. With the exception of two—an ex-collegiate boxer who ran the dorm and a crew-cut ex Marine who coached sports and ran the military drills—they were all bachelors.

Looking back, it seems clear that a majority of them were probably homosexual. The headmaster, for example, was stunningly nelly in bearing. He walked on his toes and the balls of his feet, licked his wispy lips as he scanned the room for mischief, and carried his tiny hands before him as though they pinned to his chest, palms splayed, fingers dangling, in the manner of one of the smaller carnivorous dinosaurs.

For all that, he was terrifying. His voice was high, even mincing, but it had the distilled authority of generations of no-nonsense headmistresses and formidable school-marms. For that reason, he was deferred to by both faculty and students and perhaps that is why conventional Minnesota parents entrusted their sons to his care. They, and especially the fathers among them, had been humbled, pinched, made to write sentences on the board, and given the switch on their backsides by the likes of this person. They would obey.

I suspect, in fact, that he ran a tight ship. In my time, I remember hearing of only two incidents of the staff touching the boys. (I recall at least as many teachers let go for excessive drinking). Of course, by the second of my three years there, in the seventh grade, we were busy touching ourselves and even each other. Mutual masturbation was endemic, and fellatio—often coerced by older boys on younger—not uncommon.

I was in the middle of these things and I took them in stride. I had become a good student in my classes, competent at military drill; my erotic education was proceeding apace, as was my religious formation. These seem to me today linked in some way, and I think I understood them as such at the time. I arrived at the school knowing nothing of either.

I hasten to add that the priests, deacons, and other ministers I dealt with never touched a boy that I knew of. And as an eager participant in Bible classes, acolyte duties, and every liturgy made available to us at the school, I might have known, or even—as a fatherless, sensitive, and somewhat "artistic" boy—become the object of someone's pederastic intentions. That simply never happened. On the other hand, there was scarcely a room in and around the school chapel that my friends and I had not used for mutual self-display and circle jerking. Sexual release was all the more exciting for taking place in the chapel, in the ambience of the sacred. I suppose there was a baser reckless thrill in the risk of being caught—in the frisson of lowering your pants in the sacristy, of unbuttoning your cassock on the bell tower landing to display your erection—but that was the least of it. We weren't transgressing: we were bringing ourselves, naked, that much closer to the holy; we were making an ecstatic leap.

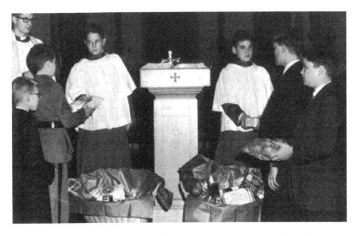

So, if anything, I brought eros with me into the church; and despite all the obvious contradictions and proscriptions to the contrary, I couldn't help feeling it belonged there—

because in my pursuit of eros I was being driven by beauty in the form of the exquisite. Or at least, that is how the sensations my body was producing felt to me. Both their origin and their aim seemed mightily powerful, greater than anything I had ever encountered intimately, at least since we'd left Bob.

That it was private and self-contained, yet scented with the transcendent—so internal and specific to me and yet so immense—made it seem a kind of answer to my prayers for connection and intimacy, for awe, and for presences and things in the world that would compensate for the losses of my first eleven years of life. I wanted—I prayed for—love and beauty, and I found them in my body and the bodies of others, and I found them in the body of Christ, in the church and its liturgy—in its rendering of desire and praise into an act of beauty—and in the God who made me and all those other bodies and presences.

This, you might say, is the thinking of a very confused young man, and I suppose you would be right. There's no visible morality or responsibility attached to it—no sense of sin or of the need to not only admire but emulate Christ—and yet, while I had no especially strong sense of shame, I felt that what I was doing was good, or at least had the capacity to make me good. I had been, I understood, a bad student and a trial to my mother, but now my grades and conduct were exemplary, and that was as far as my conception of goodness went at the time. I was a bit priggish and overweening about my religiosity, but I never imagined I was storing up points in heaven. Rather, it became simply what I liked to do—what gave me comfort and pleasure—as did my sexuality.

Of course I'd understood that sex was a secret pleasure, that it was dirty or naughty. But, once discovered, it also seemed to me a birthright, and with that I shrugged off whatever shame I might have felt. It was later, perhaps in the eighth grade, that I came to think it was wrong, or rather, that male-male sex was wrong. My appreciation of this was social and psychological rather than moral: it wasn't so much evil as odd. It made you a "pansy" or a "fairy" or a "queer" or a "homo". Now that I had the words and the contempt that colored them before me, on my lips, I finally grasped what my mother and Bon had tried to express to me eight years earlier.

For all the mockery, fear, and hatred those words contained, I understood that kids our age were granted a free pass to experiment, provided we didn't penetrate each other (known among us as "cornholing") and gave up our mutual experimentation in favor of girls once we were in high school.

I more or less followed that prescription—minus a few small slips—after I returned home to live with my mother and begin the ninth grade. My religiosity, too, seemed to fade along with the hothouse boy-with-boy eros of my early adolescence. My interest in the church ebbed increment by increment until, by age sixteen, it was entirely below the surface of my life. I never stopped believing, but for a long time I surely forgot that I believed. Perhaps I believed, but without faith, without any sense of the presence of what I believed *in*. In the same way, sex—the categorization, the obsessing, and all the bullshit and lore that adolescents trade in—took over from eros.

I had, of course, limited experience, but I did have increasingly sophisticated opinions. For example, as against the prevailing hysteria and name-calling, my friends and I began to acquire a more sophisticated and thoughtful view of homosexuality. It was a psychopathology, but I also believed that in some sense practically everyone and every family was afflicted by neurosis or even psychosis; that, in fact, the whole of American society was "fucked-up". That being the case, while you would never want to be a homosexual yourself, you might be prepared to tolerate or at least understand it in others. You might even joke about the biddies and anal retentives who worried so much about it.

There was a piece in *Mad* magazine—it was still more my bible than the Bible itself—featuring witty ripostes to common pieces of graffiti. For example, somebody was supposed to have desperately scrawled "My mother made me a homosexual" on a bathroom wall. Beneath it someone else responded, "Great! Would she make one for me too?"

It was a typical piece of mid-sixties satire, both hip to and ultimately dismissive of the antique Freudianism that underlay fears of homosexual pathology, while also on the verge of dismissing the whole notion of pathology, itself. It was a joke I loved and one I repeated with no sense of irony. But I may have been protesting too much.

Since returning home for the ninth grade, I'd been unavoidably conscious of my mother's social life. Our apartment was, by St. Paul standards, a sort of salon, its visitors much preoccupied with politics and the arts. "Boyfriends" of the kind my mother always favored were a part of it. But increasingly, my mother drew women friends (divorced, widowed, or never married), often with an interest in golf and tennis, but also possessed of a bohemian and independent cast of mind who introduced me to Billie Holiday, Lenny Bruce, and Judy Garland's *Live at Carnegie Hall* album. They were for the most part funny, appreciative of my interests and take on the world, and kind and understanding as I passed through several adolescent crises. I liked several of them as much as I have ever liked any human being.

Of course, while I'd been away, my mother had changed. Or rather she'd simply settled into a new life with new friends. I don't know to what extent she would have identified herself as bisexual or lesbian but that was, I realize now, the milieu in which she was most comfortable.

Still less would I want to speculate on whether she had lovers or on who these lovers were. But she was, I think, having the time of her life, much as I had been having under Bob's masculine influence—much as I suppose Bob was simultaneously having in the Hollywood Hills.

I, meanwhile, was lost in the way adolescents are usually lost, but perhaps in a way special to that time. In the late 1960s, when personal "realization" and "liberation" seemed so imperative, I felt I was no one in particular. I wasn't a proto-homo or an Episcopalian any more, but I wasn't anything else either. Meanwhile, it seemed to me that in other places, on campuses and on the coasts, an entirely new religion and way of life was being formed, and I could only watch it from a distance. At school, I was merely serving time; I was studiously unmotivated and unprepared. At some point in my sophomore year, I simply stopped doing the work.

When I failed half my final exams that June, the school administrators had the same advice they'd offered five years earlier: boarding school and, it went without saying, masculine influence. In the fall I found myself in rural Colorado at a school whose curriculum extended to ranching chores, mountaineering, and white water kayaking. I lasted scarcely two months before I ran away, hitchhiking to Denver, and then flying to Chicago on my TWA Youth Fare card. I read Hesse's *Siddhartha* on the plane and I wondered if the plane would crash. At O'Hare, I gave some desultory thought to trying for New York, Cambridge, San Francisco, or Berkeley, but took the last of my money and bought a ticket home to St. Paul. I was, even by my own estimation, unfit to serve in the youth revolution.

During the few days that I'd been missing, my mother's contact in Colorado was the school's Dean of Students, and after I turned up she continued to talk to him about what ought to be done with me next. I categorically refused to go back to school and my mother responded by offering me the alternative of enlisting in the service branch of my choice. That meant Vietnam, a field of battle for which I felt even less suited. I compromised by saying that I would find some way of continuing my education informally for the rest of the school year, with a view to re-enrolling somewhere, someplace, in the fall.

My mother ran this scheme past her advisor, the Dean in Colorado, who made a surprising counterproposal. Between his teaching and administrative duties, he was overburdened and had just recently been diagnosed with a heart condition. Living alone, unmarried, and without family nearby, he could hardly manage his household chores and errands without help. Would I consider becoming his assistant and valet in exchange for room, board, and private instruction in the subjects I needed to keep up with for the remainder of the school year?

I returned to Colorado in a matter of weeks. The Dean had never been my teacher during my few months at the school. But I knew about him, and perhaps he had noticed me. He taught French, Spanish, Literature, and Philosophy. He spoke three additional languages, had graduated from Columbia summa cum laude in the 1930s, and had brought old teachers and classmates like Jacques Barzun and Paul Goodman to the school. He was one of a generation of sons of Jewish immigrants who aspired to and attained academic excellence, were deeply conscious of what they'd been given, and intended to repay their debt by inculcating high culture and the classical virtues. He was warm and stern, acute and sentimental, exacting and forgiving. By my lights he might have been Socrates.

Because I was ambitious, and because I was genuinely intellectually curious, within days of arriving I grabbed *Being and Nothingness* from his bookshelves and announced I was going to read it. He didn't laugh. More usefully, I cooked spaghetti, did yard work, and made trips to the grocery store and the post office. He began to teach me French and to read Martin Buber, Thomas Mann, and Camus with me. At the end of the day, I sat with him in front of the fire. We read (I gave up on Sartre after ten or so pages) and on the phonograph the Dean worked his way through Bach and then Mozart on my behalf.

Of course we talked, often until late, and it must have been then that I heard about transcendence, of how it preoccupied Sartre and Buber and manifested itself in Mozart and Bach. Of course the talk came around to sex, among other worldly matters, and much at my behest. I am sure I strove to display my tolerance and insouciance, and he in turn told me some impressive stories of his own: how he'd run with a crowd in New York that included Aaron Copland, Leonard Bernstein, and other sexually-indefinite geniuses and artists; how he been offered a pubescent boy as a gift by a family in Morocco he'd befriended; and how it was his view that bisexuality was the natural and rational state of human affairs. I would have agreed, although I would have stated that, on balance, I preferred girls.

I could say that he put these things forward in an intentionally provocative and suggestive manner—that he was seducing me. But I know how precocious I was, and how anxious I was to prove that I was as sophisticated and self-possessed as any adult. I know, for example, that one late evening I masturbated in front of him. I could not say it was my idea, but I also know he did not encourage me. I was trying, beyond any idea or plan, to make an impression. The daring of it, the recklessness, made it sexy, of course, but also rendered it sincere, authentic, even transcendent in some way. The Dean merely sat across the room with an amused smile on his face as I showed him my youthful vigor. He neither approved nor disapproved. I suppose Socrates did much the same.

During the next few weeks, this may have happened once or twice more, but I suspect I had proved my point. We were preoccupied with other things: I, with my identity, with the need to weave my desires into a tolerable self; he, with his faltering heart. I think in our late night discussions he had told me that its fragility put scx out of bounds for him. But later he came to me with a simple request, based, he told me, on the latest advice from his cardiologist.

It was, the Dean explained, dangerous for him to have an orgasm, either during intercourse and even masturbation. The strain was too great. On the other hand, surely I understood that every man needed an occasional release of tension, a discharge of pent-up semen and sexual energies. Would I, therefore, be willing for him to come into my bed from time to time? I wouldn't have to do anything nor would he do anything beyond lying next to me. It was a matter of his health, even, I might have imagined, one of life and death.

I assented, not eagerly but dutifully. The whole business sounded reasonable but somehow odd, intimate yet sterile. The Dean didn't appear in my room for several nights, and I think I almost forgot about it. But then he came, one night after I'd already fallen asleep (it was his habit to stay up very late, reading, writing letters, and listening to Mozart) and climbed into bed behind me. I felt his erection grinding against me and then a spot of damp that he daubed away with a tuft of Kleenex. A moment later, without a word, he was gone.

This happened perhaps every two weeks over a course of several months, perhaps four or five times in all. We didn't speak about it, although he did thank me several times for my being so understanding. I didn't like these night visits, although never to such an extent that I contemplated objecting. I disliked them way I might have disliked having my temperature taken rectally (although he never attempted to penetrate me) or getting a shot or a blood test: unpleasant but medically necessary.

I think what bothered me more was that it had been the Dean's idea rather than mine, that he'd trumped the erotic powers I'd displayed to him with his own more serious needs. I may also have worried that he was making a homo out of me, although since our contact was both passive on my part and consciously undesired by me, I wasn't overly troubled. On the other hand, I felt there was something a little noble in my subjecting myself to his medical needs, a sense of Christian sacrifice, of yielding at my own expense, and so what I lost in psychopathological terms I gained in spiritual ones.

Still, I left Colorado earlier than I'd planned, but on perfectly friendly terms. I went east to investigate schools I might attend the next year near my relatives in Massachusetts. The Dean and I kept up a steady correspondence and talked on the phone occasionally as I

entered my senior year of high school. He seemed
genuinely interested in my future and hoped I would do
something worthwhile with my intellectual gifts. He hoped
I would remember what he'd tried to teach me about
culture and the virtues.

Throughout high school I'd dated, attended dances, and
done some making out with girls, but I'd never gotten
much past deep kissing, writhing and grinding, and several
breasts cupped through a layer of mohair. But in senior
year, I became aggressively—what would later be called
performatively—heterosexual: I would swim into the
deeper water of heavy petting and beyond, or drown
trying.

I made some progress. I saw my first bare breast in the
woods of a summer camp where I worked that summer.
And then I saw another. Later, in the winter, I felt around
inside a girl's jeans, and I was chagrined to hear from a
mutual friend that she had been disappointed I hadn't try to
go "further". But I never succeeded in arranging a return
engagement with her, or in moving towards "further" with
other girls. Neither, of course, were most of my friends and
acquaintances. Sexual frustration is the daily bread of male
adolescence, but in my mouth it tasted of ashes.

I feared that what had happened with the Dean—or
perhaps even back in Junior High—had become a kind of
destiny, that if I wasn't a homosexual by pathology, I'd
become one by default. My mother hadn't needed to make
me a homosexual: I'd done it myself.

In the spring I wrote the Dean a letter. The term
"abuse" wasn't in wide use yet, certainly not tied to the
word "sexual", nor were many "victims" in evidence, never
mind "survivors". But that wasn't what I wanted to say. I
simply needed to declare that what we—and especially he,
with me—had done was wrong: not in general, I took pains

to say, but wrong for *me*. It was not who I was and I wanted him to know and understand that.

I know my tone must have been strident and self-important to a fault. I didn't hear back from the Dean for perhaps six weeks—he was ordinarily a prompt, not to say fastidious, correspondent. Finally a letter arrived: he'd been traveling and then had undergone some incidents regarding his health about which he would fill me in later.

Then he turned to the matter of my last letter. He called it "brave" and "forthright" and "mature". But he concluded, "I think you still misunderstand the sexual aspects of your stay here and why I permitted you to do some of the things that were done." He closed by wishing me a happy high school graduation and offering his hope that the pride he took in me would be justified.

I was not happy with this response. It seemed to put matters exactly upside down, and to condescend to me in the process. He had focused, I supposed, completely on my self-exhibition and forgotten about his own nocturnal visits to my bed. Or did it mean that those, too, were things he had "permitted [me] to do", that I'd somehow *meant* to happen?

I was perplexed and angry and I needed to straighten this out with him. My identity—the case I was making for myself of being one thing and not another—was at stake. But the Dean had the last word. Before I had the chance to write back, he died of a massive heart attack. But he was, after all, called the Dean by dint of being wiser than any of his students, and perhaps most of all me. He left me a puzzle that I had to figure out on my own, not the least of which was the question of what happened to faith, love, and beauty in the face of this new acquaintance, this eternal being called death.

I attempted that over many years, among bodies and hearts, navigating my own desires and the boundaries of others, in the places where these matters are rightly worked out. For all the hurt and confusion that occurred, I am glad I did it during that time rather than more recently. I'm glad I did not cast the Dean in the role as my abuser and myself as the innocent survivor of his evil. For I was not remotely innocent. I knew that myself, back from the time I began to go to chapel in the sixth grade. I knew I was lonely, broken, and full of want. I needed saving.

It would have been better, of course, if the Dean had stayed out of my bed, if he had not insulted his own considerable intelligence by concocting the lame story of his need to ejaculate on my sixteen-year-old buttocks for the sake of his heart. But perhaps the matter was, after all, his heart. Perhaps he loved me as Bob loved Ted: blindly, deceitfully, and unwisely.

My mother put me in his path: his and Bob's and the boarding school and then, later, her own female friends, who were the inverse, the photographic negative, of all those gay men. But then she also put me in the way of art— art understood as a kind of intimacy with the created and the tragic—and, through that, of faith: faith on account of doubt, on account of a life so lacking in sureties that the doubt it engendered had no choice but intermittently to effloresce into faith, however quickly it might flame out. And I loved them all, the men and the boys and the women and the whole world that came with them. That was my choice.

My mother might have thought she could make me a homosexual, and if the authoritative, homophobic science of her time had been correct, she might by her folly have succeeded. Of course the science was wrong, and her worst sin was not to know her own mind or to mistake her own heart's desire, which is no sin at all. It was the same fault that afflicted us all: her, Bob, the Dean, and me, too. That, and wanting what we believed we loved, which is no more than our nature.

As it turned out, I am heterosexual. It might have been otherwise, in this matter as in any other, with me or with any of us. Suppose my mother had loved men a little more, or loved a different sort of man; or suppose Bob had loved her rather than Ted; and suppose I had not been so willful and sad a child, or that I had liked Bob and his dogs a little less; or that the Dean hadn't died, and I had loved him, and was just now—when he was very old—putting him in his grave? But it is like this, not that.

The Dean was the first adult in my life whom I knew as something like an adult who died. When I began to pray again—in a derisory way—some years ago, I included him in my prayers. It was without regard for what had happened between us, for what he may have intended towards me or how I felt about it. It's no real sacrifice; much less than that involved in his permitting me to do the things that were done. I know he was important to me, and it is the only way I know how to keep his presence in my life, to insist on his existence.

I prayed, too, for my mother and Bob. They are both dead now: my mother of natural causes, and Bob of causes rather less so, or perhaps especially natural to him. When I was in college in California, I looked up Bob in the phone book and there he was. It was surprisingly easy. We still liked each other. He was openly gay and I was openly straight. I held my wedding reception at his house in Benedict Canyon. There, he met my mother for the first time in almost twenty years.

Later, because we had become very frank with one another, he confessed that he was surprised by how much her looks and dress sense had declined. "She had style," he said, almost wistfully. "She had pizzazz."

For my part, I wondered why she didn't remarry. My sister and I both felt she shouldn't spend her old age alone. Of course, the nature of her true sexual preferences— of what, perhaps, *her* mother had made her—didn't even occur to me. In that, I was an innocent. One day with Bob, thinking aloud, I wondered why she had never gotten together with Henry Smith, for whom she had apparently carried a torch since high school.

"My dear," Bob hooted, "Henry Smith brought me *out* when I was sixteen."

Later, Bob and I went into business together fixing up and reselling derelict houses. Initially, we used his capital, but then, when I received a bequest from my grandfather's will, we went in on a house fifty/fifty. A few days after we'd gutted it, Bob left a bar, much the worse for wear, in order to follow home someone he'd met there. Not seeing a red light, he struck another car head-on. Its occupants walked away unscathed, but Bob's body—he wasn't belted in—leapt from the seat. The top of his skull was thrown through the windshield.

I sat next to him for some weeks in a neurology intensive care unit. Unconscious, in a coma, he looked like the Tin Man in *The Wizard of Oz*, his head shaved with a drainage tube coming out the top through a funnel-shaped shunt. I wondered if the duty nurses who dealt with his catheter had commented to each other on his penis. I'd seen it once and, about that, he hadn't lied to my mother.

After a time, when the neurologists said he was past hope, I helped the brother who hated him move Bob to a shabby welfare-recipient nursing home. He hadn't had any money to speak of in his accounts; they held a fraction of what he'd led me to believe when I agreed to go in on the latest house project. I had to finish that with my own funds. Moreover, since I'd co-signed a loan document with Bob that contained something called a cross-collateral clause, it turned out I was responsible for other debts of his I didn't even know existed. So went my grandfather's legacy and much more.

The last time I saw Bob, who had never regained consciousness, he was in that state nursing home, perhaps a year or two before he finally died. He was on his side, curling up upon himself, not just his trunk and his legs, but his head and his neck. His hands had become frail and delicate talons. I could not feel angry about the spot he'd left me in. He was a known quantity and I should have known better. I couldn't hate him. Anyway, now, since the accident, he'd paid and paid and paid. What a waste.

It might have been otherwise. I suppose he had met someone beautiful that night, someone as handsome as Ted. He might have thought he'd seen God in that stranger's eyes, in the composure of the limbs and torso, and he'd lost his balance, driving when he ought to have known better. He launched himself at this new body, at the chance to love it; and intent on the stranger's taillights, mistaking the way, fell   shrieking   into   Beauty's—his   Maker's—embrace.

3.
DARKROOM

Before all that, before sex and my discovery of its infinite, joyous, furtive varieties, of how we suffer for it, I was baptized. I was eleven years old, a sixth grader attending an Episcopalian boarding school in southern Minnesota. It was two days after Christmas (there was a hard, crunching snow on the ground) and thirty-five days after the assassination of John Kennedy. My mother and maternal grandparents were present. There were three witnesses and godparents and two priests: the rector of my grandparents' parish, St. John's in St. Paul, where the ceremony was taking place, and the chaplain of my school.

According to the certificate, which I still have, I promised "to renounce the devil and all his works, the pomps and vanity of this wicked world, and all the sinful lusts of the flesh" as well as to believe "all the articles of the Christian faith" and "to keep God's holy will and commandments, and to walk in the same all the days of my life". Then water must have poured on my head, followed by a prayer, and there would have been congratulations all around. My mother had been in rebellion against her parents' religion when I was born, but now I—unbidden and of my own free will—had entered the fold. It was an unexpected and gratifying event for my grandparents, and, I suspect, a relief to my mother, a vicarious mending of an interfamilial schism.

But I remember none of that with any clarity. I only remember the angel. She was life-sized, or at least—since I

have no idea how large angels actually are—of human scale
and proportion. She had waves of hair falling down her neck
and a gown belted just below her breasts that pooled in
folds and drapes around her sandaled feet. She held an
enormous scallop shell and this held the water with which I
was baptized. She seemed to be gazing down into this,
pensive but serene in her beauty.

I was most struck, however, by her color and what I
can only call the texture of her body. The angel was made
of white stone, neither dull nor shiny, but crystalline like
salt or sugar or new snow. Whatever the light gave it—and
I later realized several flood lamps artfully lighted it—it
seemed to give back translucently, as though radiated from
within itself. At the time I imagined this was alabaster,
which I knew from singing "America the Beautiful" was an
exquisite material, although I now suspect it was some
more modest type of stone.

I think that the quality she held for me had to do with
the light; almost with what I don't want to call "a trick of
the light". The angel seemed in any case a being that I
wanted to get closer to. I had an irresistible urge to be with
her, but in what way was unclear: as mother, girlfriend,
guardian, or savior, or perhaps some combination of all of
them.

I don't know exactly what had taken hold of me, no
more than I do what possessed me in wanting to be
baptized. Perhaps it was simply to get within proximity of
the angel. I can't recall asking to be baptized, but at the
same time I'm quite clear it was done at my request and
that it was done in a hurry.

In September that same year, three months earlier, I'd
begun attending a school affiliated with the Episcopal
Church. Chapel was required twice a week, but beyond
that there was little religious observance and certainly no
attempt to proselytize. I know I was impressed by the

liturgy, which, although distinctly "low" church, was as theatrical as anything I'd seen, and I know I was moved by the sound of the hymns, plainsong, and organ as well as of the Prayer Book's Tudor English. I also suppose that, like any sixth grader, I simply wanted to belong, and although only half the students were Episcopalian, that was another means of fitting in at a new school.

What I can't find is any evidence of fervor, of that "change of heart" Evangelicals speak of, never mind of being "born again". That, of course, was not the manner of Episcopalianism, which true to its English roots, makes an outward show of pomp and ceremony but is inwardly and psychologically restrained, even reticent. Perhaps, for other reasons, it went without saying: my parents had separated when I was one year old, and my father contracted polio shortly thereafter. I saw him twice thereafter, during court-ordered visitations. He lay on his bed, breathing through a respirator, scarcely able to move his head from side to side. He had died five years before my baptism and perhaps, however heavy-handed and obvious the interpretation may be, I simply wanted to replace him with a stronger, more powerful, or at least more reliable father.

Still, I have the weekly letters I wrote home all that autumn and winter, and the baptism is never mentioned, before or after the fact. The closest I came to displaying any newfound religiosity is in wishing my mother "Happy Advent". I do remember being excited to discover the existence of this season before Christmas, and how I liked the purple altar furnishings and vestments and especially the Advent wreath, whose four candles were lighted on successive Sundays, counting down to Christmas Day.

Of course any child anticipates Christmas with an almost erotic longing, and perhaps my observance of Advent made the anticipation that much more delicious. My letters do mention the things I wanted for Christmas: a book of Indian lore, a record store gift certificate, a biology class dissection set, but most of all a used 35mm camera. I'd had a succession of Brownies and then an Instamatic, but the 35mm was real camera, the kind my grandfather used to take his Kodachrome slides. That the camera I had my eye on was made by an obscure manufacturer and had a cracked viewfinder did nothing to lessen my ardor.

As against the clouded memory of my baptism, I recall precisely what I did with my new camera: I went and photographed my grandparent's church in Ektachrome. I'd heard it was the color film professionals preferred, rather than the Kodachrome my Grandfather used for his family line-ups and tedious cloudscapes and sunsets; the kind of things I intended to surpass. I took shots of the sanctuary, its white and gold altar cloths, its garlands of spruce and pine, and the blue winter light bleeding through the stained glass windows. And of course I shot the angel from several angles. In the slides, however, her immaculate white body came out a discolored ivory, tending to orange. That, too, was a trick of the light.

Early in January I sent some prints of these to the rector, Reverend Mead, who had baptized me. This is the only allusion to that event in my letters home for the rest of the year. On the other hand, the letters are full of talk about photography, of requests for film, prints, and photography magazines. A lot of kids took pictures at my school, and there was even a rudimentary darkroom we were allowed to use. They were shutterbugs toting Brownies and Instamatics, but with my 35mm I was already thinking of myself as someone working at a higher, more serious level. I set my mind to photography with the same willful deliberation I had with religion.

My original model of a photographer was my grandfather, the first person I'd ever seen with a camera that f-stops and shutter speeds and produced slides rather than snapshots. He was, in reality, the very essence of an amateur. There were no imperatives to his photography beyond his own pleasure and a need to reify again and again a repertoire of clichés: the family face-forward, the spectacular sunset, the antic child, the capering or solicitous pet, the adult raising a convivial glass to the lens.

Of course their technical deficiencies were manifold, but my grandfather had no particular expectations. If a shot "turned out" it was a serendipitous stroke of luck like a run of good cards at the bridge table. In the same spirit his photographs were barely composed or even framed. He aimed at the center of the cluster of aunts, uncles, and cousins and flung his dart. If it landed within the boundaries of the print or slide frame he was happy enough. He accepted and perhaps even cultivated the givenness of his images, the vagaries of blinking subjects, uncertain focal lengths, unbalanced, excessive, or inadequate light. Whatever came back from the photo lab was gratefully received.

Once I had my own 35mm camera, I imagined I would quickly overtake my grandfather, but there was nothing to bear that pretension out in my photos. In terms of composition and formal interest, they scarcely equaled my Grandfather's Kodachromes. I took pictures of boys from school pitching rocks into the river, of baseball plays obscured and blurred by a frieze of chain-link fence, and of a bend in a pair of railroad tracks arcing off to their vanishing point.

I also habitually photographed church interiors: long shots up the aisle towards the altar, stone tablets and memorials, and stained glass windows. But for all my effort, these were the most disappointing of my photographs: for lack of light, they lacked contrast and detail; or because I was using daylight film under artificial light and knew nothing of tungsten film or filters, the colors were bleached or luridly flared.

Despite that, I kept at it, oblivious to my photos technical flaws and the sheer dullness of their content and composition. I was devoted to the work, religiously so, and I suppose I believed it constituted something allied to the transcendent and the beautiful, to art.

I was also, in the manner of self-conceived geniuses, ambitious. I persuaded my grandparents to let me set up a darkroom in an abandoned coal cellar in their basement and to outfit it with a twenty-year old used enlarger. It was corroded to begin with, but in the damp of the cellar it began to rust. The technical faults in my photographs multiplied: my negatives were fogged by light leaks into my darkroom, stained and marred by tired chemicals, inadequate rinsing, and poor temperature control, and scratched by particles of the omnipresent coal dust. My prints weren't any better: muddy, blanched, or milky in tone and spotted with dust and crud that had lodged inside the enlarger.

But I went on, undeterred. I was brazen. In the seventh grade I took photos of my schools sports teams—the football squad vaguely out of focus, the basketball players eerily lupine on account of red-eye from my flash—and talked the members and their fans into buying them. That spring I learned that perhaps the most eminent photographer in the state lived not a block from my family in a large stone house, and one afternoon during the summer between the seventh and eight grades, I simply went to his door and knocked. The house was imposing in the manner of most of the houses on that street, our city's premier boulevard, but conspicuous for having a bright red door —crimson in fact. It was opened by a small, hunched old figure with a crabbed and harried expression, the kind of man who spoons out the castor oil in an orphanage. I was afraid, but forced myself to ask if the photographer were in. He was, the old man allowed, and shut the door in my face, presumably to go fetch him.

Some time later, the door opened again and in it stood a younger man, perhaps forty-five or fifty. His hair was combed back over his head and he had a pencil mustache. He wore an ascot and a white shirt that seemed to balloon around his shoulders and arms. A cigarette dangled from his mouth. But it was the crutches that startled me; those and, as he motioned me to come in and turned down the hall, his rolling, corkscrewed walk. He might have been sawed in half at the hips and then put back together again with the halves slightly misaligned. I was not sure it was a good idea to go inside, but I followed.

We entered the kitchen where the old man was preparing lunch. The photographer indicated that this was his father, who looked up, glowered at me, and returned to agitating his pan of tomato soup. The photographer lowered himself into a canvas director's chair, and as he did, he pitched the crutches toward the wall where, miraculously, they settled, leaning upright. Then he drew hard on his cigarette, and asked me what he could do for me.

It had not occurred to me to formulate an answer to this in advance. I wanted to learn about photography, I said. I hoped I could hang around and see what I could learn. It only strikes me now how audacious, not to say presumptuous, this was, as though I were oblivious to the fact that this was a grown-up with a life to lead, with a business to run. And I suppose, in truth, I was oblivious to that and much more. The old man brought the photographer a bowl of soup and a plate of toast.

He stubbed out his cigarette and began his lunch. At some point, he asked if I wanted something to eat, but I thought it better not to impose nor, more crucially, to chance the old man's cooking. Then it came out that, yes, the photographer might be able to help me out. At a minimum, he'd be happy to show me around his studio.

He hauled himself up and onto his crutches, crutches I saw were fabricated of stainless steel and black rubber, as slender and elegant as crutches might be. As I followed him out of kitchen and from one room to the next, it seemed that this house was very much like my grandparents' house a few blocks down the same street: constructed on three floors on the same broad and massive lines, with its formal, high-ceilinged downstairs giving onto a central foyer and staircase by means of double doors. There was a dumbwaiter, a backstairs, and an indicator board in the hall for a now moribund system of bells and call buttons. It was a house designed in the 1890s for a prosperous family and its servants, but now it contained only the photographer and his sour old father.

But for their two bedrooms and the kitchen, it was otherwise consecrated entirely to photography. What had once been the living room was an enormous studio cluttered with lights and three cameras—eight-by-ten and five-by-seven Linhof view cameras and a two-and-a-quarter Hasselblad— on tripods. From the ceiling hung long rolls of background paper in four or five colors. Cables ran over the oak floor and the windows were blacked-out. The adjacent dining room was outfitted with a dry-mounting press, board and paper cutters, and racks of boxed prints and illustration board. In what my grandparents would have termed the library or parlor another studio was set up for seated portraits and groups.

I was impressed by these rooms and a little intimidated by their being sealed off from daylight, lit only by the fill and strobe lights in their standby setting. But I wasn't much interested in studio photography. I wanted to see the Hasselblad and the 35mm Nikons, if he had any (which of course he did), the tools of photojournalism and art photography. More than these, I wanted to see his darkroom.

In fact, the photographer told me, he had two darkrooms, one in the basement to process film and another upstairs for printing. And with that he seated himself on the stair lift parallel to the balustrade and, with me climbing the stairs alongside him, we ascended.

The darkroom was adjacent to his bedroom at the back of the second floor, and was entered by a sort of lightproof airlock. Inside, the walls, ceiling, and floor were painted black. There was a long bank of sinks along one wall in which trays sat surrounded by a continuous flow of temperature-controlled water. Above it were fixed shelves filled with jars and jugs of chemicals.

An outsized bench against the adjacent wall held two enlargers (one for the sheet film from the view cameras, another for the 35mm and two-and-a-quarter negatives), long with timers, controllers, and switches. Beneath and to one side of it were boxes upon boxes of photographic paper in different sizes, grades, and finishes, and a little further off to one side a phonograph and a stack of jazz and classical record albums. The photographer also had a special chair, a tall stool on wheels upon which he could scoot himself back and forth between the enlargers and the developing trays using one crutch.

After he'd shown me the layout of the darkroom, the photographer threw a switch. For an instant, the room was utterly black, without any light, so dark that the darkness felt almost material, a substance through which you might slowly and laboriously pick your way. But then a half dozen bell-shaped lamps suspended from the ceiling went on. They cast brownish-orange pools of illumination over the sinks and the enlarger bench, a light by which you could see but which seemed to give no shadows or depth to the objects it fell upon, an airless light by which you could work as though underwater.

I was a little relieved when the photographer put the regular lights back on, but no less thrilled by what I had seen: a darkroom more fabulous than any I could have imagined. It was not only magnificent, it was a cool—a quality I had just lately begun to grasp and which was exceedingly rare in Minnesota. In fact, the photographer was cool: it was cool that he had a mustache, that he wore outsized shirts, that he had oil paintings on his walls—real ones, abstracts on canvas—and that the walls and hallways themselves were painted dark olive green and Chinese red and were lit by floods and spots that left vast pools of shadow and dark, not spooky dark but cool dark.

Most adults I knew were authoritarian—the character of their relation with me was explicitly or implicitly about control—and when they relaxed they were earnest or dull: they either kept their true selves hidden, or perhaps they had no selves of any real interest to see. They were, in the argot of the day, uptight, or, as psychologists liked to put it, anal.

But the photographer was offhand; as in the style of his twisted body, he was all akimbo. He didn't care if I was under control. He had time for me, me and his darkroom. What he cared about, it seemed, was his art. I sensed all this as we went back downstairs, as he sidewinded his way down the hall, onto his perch on the chairlift, and returned to the kitchen, where I asked him if I could come back and he said I could. And I knew it, grasped it incontrovertibly, as I walked past his garage and saw his car: a black 1958 Thunderbird.

His polio, his sickness and the handicap it had incised on his body, had of course struck me, but less as a fact than a faint presence, a backlight against which his other qualities—the thing he had made of his life—contrasted and even shone. Nor can I say that I made a conscious connection between my father and him, between the ashes of my father's history and the triumph of the photographer's, who had turned his tragedy into art in even the simplest things, in his insouciant clothes and dark, transgressive automobile.

≈

I spent much of that summer at the photographer's. Sometimes he or the old man had to send me away when a subject was being photographed in the studio or there was a backlog of work in the darkroom. But as the weeks passed, he began to allow me to stand around as he worked. I was learning to be quiet and how and when to fetch things he needed, or to run errands, tasks for which I could be his "legs". I ate the old man's cooking at lunch, and although I never stopped believing he disliked me, he seemed to scowl at me less.

I also began to learn something of the photographer's history. He had gotten polio during the Depression, and had spent several years in a hospital ward recovering and learning to breathe and walk again. It was there that he took up photography, studying by correspondence course. He had been married once. He was from South Dakota. That was as much he told me.

I tried to find out more. I was a snoop, and the fact that the photographer couldn't move very fast—that in fact you could hear the squeak and sigh of him approaching on his crutches—allowed me to enter his private rooms for brief periods without being detected. His bedroom was just opposite the entrance to the upstairs darkroom. He kept it dark with the shades pulled down, even in the height of summer, and it was black and sumptuous. There was a red cover on the bed and a rank of overstuffed orange and black pillows at its head. I am sure the nightstands and the dresser were Chinese or Japanese, or at least wrought in a style I was unfamiliar with. The details of the room are difficult to recall, perhaps because it was hard to see them in the first place.

I do know there were record albums and art books (some of them featuring nudes) and copies of Playboy (a publication whose images, tattered and passed around among boys I knew, I had taken consolation in, but which was never openly displayed in the homes I frequented). A small stand held liquor, glasses, and an ice bucket. And there were photographs hanging on the walls and set atop most of the tables and counter spaces. Most of these were of women and, I realized over time, of one woman in particular.

I was not much past the age when a boy's benchmark for female beauty is his mother, or perhaps a favorite aunt, but this woman I quickly realized was more beautiful than any woman I had known. She was film-star beautiful, yet more beautiful than a film star for not being one; for being someone you might know, or at least someone the photographer had known. I also saw from the signatures in the corners and from what I was beginning to comprehend as the photographer's style that they were all his work, that he had photographed her again and again.

The woman's face was serene, dignified yet—I would have said had I known the word—sensuous. She had high cheekbones, large eyes (brown I would have ventured, although all the photos were in black and white), and her nose was of a piece with her chin, straight and—again, had I known the word—classical. The photographer's style was a little in the mode of Hollywood portrait photography of the 1940s, and his rendering of this woman made her a little sweeter than Barbara Stanwyk but more severe than Rita Hayworth.

But I am not sure that her hair was not more significant than her face. Again, I had to extrapolate the color from the gray of the print: medium brown or even auburn. But the color was the least of it, because it wasn't merely hair—a

superfluity that might be altered or shortened without
changing the person who wore it—but an integral part of
her. It was sculptural in the way that Bernini's drapery is no
less essential to his figures than are their hands or ecstatic
lips. The woman's hair had folds or pleats, but it had mass,
and in the way it fell and flowed off and around the head, it
had gravity, a kind of downward motion.

But for all that it was a little insubstantial. You might
have said that the hair and indeed the whole face was
slightly out of focus, but not so much that you might squint
to see if you could make it out more clearly. Rather, the
forms contained in the photograph were not so much
blurred as they were diffuse, or as though being seen
through some diffuse material—a veil or lightly frosted
glass or a diaphanous mist.

I knew from looking in the studio that the photographer
used various filters and that in the dark room he had not
only the customary tools for producing dodges, burns, and
vignette effects, but also sheets of glass he laid right over
the photographic paper on the enlarger easel to produce
scarcely   perceptible   patterns—crystalline,   linear,
pointillist—in the finished print. Everything that went on in
the darkroom was a kind of etching with light, of masking
and exposing the coating of silver on the paper so that some
places darkened and others did not, an illumination but also
corruption since what darkened the paper and thereby
threw the images into relief, into visibility, was chemically
not much different from the tarnishing of silver.

But the images of the woman were just as much or
more a product of lighting in the studio: of calculating not
only the shadows and highlights a given arrangement of
lamps might make fall on a subject, but of the perceived
sense of distance and volume—what became the presence
of the person pictured—that the light induced in the eye of
the viewer.

In that sense, it was the light that was material and the body and face of the subject that was immaterial; the light that was solid and the flesh that was transparent. It was this that gave the images their air of sharpness within diffusion, of seeming to be renderings of spirit rather than matter, of angels rather than creatures, an impression of a numinous sculpture cast in light and poured in silver.

I could not help but think the photographer must have loved this woman very deeply to have photographed her so many times. Perhaps he felt compelled to, if only on account of her beauty. I suppose he was lucky to have such a fine model, and in that sense he was merely using her, practicing his art upon her. Having never seen her in the flesh, I could not say if he had succeeded in capturing her beauty completely, or if perhaps he had exceeded it; had made her still more beautiful than she was in reality, in ordinary life. In any case, because of love or obsession or artistic ambition—perhaps all three—he had taken great care, great pains, and immeasurable time and concentration with her.

There was also a photograph of the woman in the hallway, and one afternoon that August I made a pretense of noticing it and asked the photographer who it was. "She was my wife," he said and offered nothing more. I understood it was something he didn't want to go into, not only with me but perhaps with anyone. From then on, I felt that this woman rather than his polio had been the great tragedy of his life. Her leaving him (perhaps because of the polio and what it had done to his body) or their not being able to get along was the great shadow that overlaid the entire house, that adhered to its every corner, that made the darkroom— where the photographer mustered such light as he could through the enlarger's lens—dark.

I can't say I thought of that or of the photographer himself much once I returned to school in the fall. I'd stumbled onto my sexuality—masturbation and sex with other boys—and with it, images of my own to incite, prolong, and deepen it. I did visit the photographer during the Christmas holidays. There was no wreath on the door and no tree inside the house. In the studio and the darkrooms his winter days were identical to the summer. The days were shorter, but the amplitude of light and dark inside the house was the same.

For Christmas that year, I got an unusually large check from my grandparents and I used it, together with a vast advance on my allowance, to buy a used two-and-a-quarter reflex camera. I took it back to school in January, ran a dozen rolls of film through it, and submitted my new work—not much less execrable than before—to our school yearbook. Some of them were used on a page of student "candids", and so I was at last in print, reproduced and set before an audience of perhaps hundreds.

The following summer, on the cusp of ninth grade, of high school and true adolescence, the photographer became a little freer with me. He didn't treat me as an equal or reveal anything more of himself, but that he let me do more around the house and included me in his work. We filled the black Thunderbird with cases and light stands and went out. I helped him—if only as a porter and errand boy—photograph new skyscrapers and the gubernatorial candidates of that year's election. He began to let me work on my own projects in his darkroom when he wasn't busy there.

I could have learned a great deal just by watching him pose his subjects, arrange his lights, angle his tripod, filter his lenses, and choose the precise moment to trip the shutter. But I didn't. It wasn't that I was unobservant or didn't listen, and I certainly knew how good he was: I bragged to my friends about knowing him. Rather, his best work seemed beyond anything I might achieve in the near future—it was part of the miraculous word of grown-up competence that had mastered the slide rule and sent astronauts into space—and I was indifferent to the more quotidian kinds of photography that were his bread and butter.

For example, it wasn't until that second summer that I realized he had taken my mother's wedding portrait. I was looking through an album, and there, in the right hand corner, was his signature. At the home of my grandparents, who kept a kind of photographic shrine to their children on a table in the living room, I saw he had also photographed my aunts as brides. The wedding portraits were all full length, the gown a whorl spreading out from the feet, the head lit from above. Their objects floated like the Columbia Pictures' logo goddess with her torch.

I'd been looking at these photos since I was four or five, and I could have pictured any one of them accurately in my mind's eye. But I'd seen them as one sees an icon, not as a representation *of* someone but almost as the person themselves, a fragment or trace of their actual presence. You would say, "That's Aunt Patsy", not "that's an image of Aunt Patsy", and so it—she—was. How or by whom it was made was beside the point, of no interest. As family talismans—as signs that manifested the bodies of its members—neither the idea of art nor of the artist was really applicable.

But now that I was a photographer myself, I looked as these relics and icons in a different light. To discover in them evidence that the photographer's world—the house and the darkroom and his obscure existence—had intersected with mine, with its flesh and blood, seemed stunning and profound.

I mentioned to him one day in June that I had seen these portraits, complimented him on their quality—although in truth they had none of the distinction of his images of his ex-wife—and pressed him on whether he recollected anything about the sessions at which they were shot. The photographer responded vaguely to my query, but I couldn't imagine that anyone could photograph my mother and not take away some impression beyond the negatives that he supposed must be filed away somewhere. That he had probably shot at least a couple of portraits a week for the last twenty years did not occur to me.

Nor could I fathom that he wasn't as curious about my family and me as I was about him. But he disclosed himself in the same manner as he might have made a print: selectively dodging, manipulating presence and absence in a dialectic of light and dark which never composed itself into an image. He was a shadowy figure.

I also couldn't square his offhand reaction to these forgotten photographs to the ideas his work had engendered in me about art: the seriousness and passion that drove you to it and to the deep and consequential truths it manifested. I think I must have imagined that my mother's beauty should have prompted him to do great things.

I had such notions about my own photography. I was already becoming a snob about commercial work, but I couldn't grasp that the photographer's old portraits of my family had been for him nothing more than that. Even my new reflex camera wasn't serious—I want to say "grave"— enough for me, and in early July I persuaded the photographer to loan me a five-by-seven view camera with bellows and an enormous ground glass focusing screen you monitored from under a black cape. I took it, of course, to church.

Not just any church, however. By then I was after some grander, more serious conception of religion, and the church I was baptized in seemed, like my smaller cameras, incommensurate with my yearnings. So I took the view camera to the Catholic Cathedral of St. Paul. For all my presumption and general cheekiness, I entered the building a little fearfully, firstly, because I wasn't sure I had any business taking photographs there; secondly because I wasn't a Catholic, which meant that perhaps I shouldn't be in the cathedral at all. Now I tend to believe that the photography was an excuse to be in the building—to poke around in a place I felt I shouldn't be but wanted to enter into.

It was a daunting church, huge in fact, as big as our state capitol that sat on an adjacent hill. The Catholic Church itself was a daunting institution, ancient, immense, and, to a Protestant, both mysterious and suspect. In scale and in form, it catered to the senses—it traded in superfluities of awe and pity—and that was precisely what drew me to it. It was intense and overwrought, Gothic and Baroque where Protestantism was lean and neo-classical. Its surfaces—the censers, chant, and plethora of rites, saints, and hierarchies—extended to unimaginable depths and heights. At just that time the erotic had welled up in me like an efflorescence of acne, and I could not have told you where that craving ended and this one—both all about beauty and being swept away towards some ultimate kind of being— began.

The first day I made an exterior shot from a little way down the hill. It was hot and humid, and as though from the day itself, a flare of light or fog got in through the negative carrier. It bleached out the image but created a corona over the dome of the cathedral. My second exterior—taken from a closer vantage point—wasn't fogged, but it was slightly out-of-focus and lopped the cupola off the top of the dome.

But it was the interior I was after and I hauled my gear inside. I didn't ask anyone permission. I simply set my camera up on its tripod and worked as quickly as I could, hoping I would be viewed as just another tourist taking a snapshot. I managed a straight-on view of the High Altar and another from the side before retreating. A service was about to begin, and I had already gotten away with plenty. I wasn't going to intrude on the mass, or, worse, be mistaken for a worshipper.

The next day I processed the film in the photographer's basement darkroom and then, when the negatives were dry, he allowed me to print them on the enlarger upstairs. I sat in the dark on the photographer's tall, wheeled stool and watched the images form themselves, pooling into a mosaic of grays in the developing tray under the russet safelight.

I made one print and then another, and when I was done I felt triumphant. These were serious works made with serious equipment for serious reasons. I wanted to dry mount them on illustration board so I could exhibit them and carry them around in a portfolio. The photographer helped me do this without any comment about the pictures. It was not his way to comment, to cast light where none was wanted.

Doubtless he saw what I could or would not see: that every one of the photos had some technical fault, not to speak of defects of craft, never mind of art. He did explain the problem of the top of the baldachin being out of focus in my straight-on shot of the High Altar. This was an architectural camera I had been using, he emphasized, and both the lens mount and the back that held the film could be tilted so as to allow the correction of foreshortening and to deal with the problem that the base of a building might be in focus while its pinnacle was not. But you had to know what you were doing: you had, for example, to keep those two planes parallel. He did not speak the words, but it went without saying that I did not know what I was doing in this regard, or in many, many others.

I think he was wise not to say so, although I no more knew his reasons than I did the fate of his wife and his marriage. I was eager to learn, of course, but no one could tell me anything I was unprepared to hear once I was set on a course as serious as this one. He might as well have tried to talk me out of pursuing beauty or giving up masturbation or resisting the gravities that were pulling me toward the Catholic Church.

I went back to the cathedral a day later. This time I set up my camera in the apse that formed a half circle behind the High Altar. It gave on to the sacristy and, on either side, a succession of small altars dedicated to various saints and martyrs. I photographed several of these and, working my way toward the sacristy door, peaked inside. It was here that all the ceremonial gear—vestments, candlesticks, censers, and liturgical silver—were housed. A young priest saw me and asked me what I was doing. Terrified, I admitted I was "looking around", taking a few photographs.

The priest told me to come in if I wanted. He was preparing for the noon mass, and his vestments were laid on top of an enormous chest into which were set a rank of shallow drawers that might have held maps or blueprints. I shuffled further into the sacristy and saw there was also a boy inside it, a boy about my age dressed in a cassock and surplice. He looked at me sullenly, or so it seemed to me.

I asked the priest what was in the drawers, and he pulled a couple open to reveal further sets of vestments, more or less identical to the green ones on top of the chest but in other colors, purple, red, and white. Then he began to dress. There were a series of prayers printed on a card that sat on the chest, and as he donned each piece of his ensemble he said these under his breath. When he had finished, he and the boy waited for the noon bell to strike. I felt no sense that they were engaged in anything of great importance. They might, except for their clothing, have been about to go fishing or to toss a baseball back and forth.

I excused myself. I wanted to get away before the mass began. But back in the apse, I met another priest, this one smaller but attired in a soutane with a red piping, buttons, and a skullcap and sash, a bishop. Having negotiated the sacristy without embarrassment or harm, I was by now less afraid and it didn't seem he was going to confront or even speak to me. But drawing from some reservoir of chutzpah I wasn't conscious of possessing, I spoke to him. I asked him if I could take his picture.

He was on his way somewhere, in a hurry. But he agreed and stood in front of one of small altars. I took one shot, and persuaded him to stand still for another. Then he was gone.

I packed up my gear, exultant. I had made a full-length portrait of a prelate in his habitat, a genuine bishop. It was apotheosis of my work in the cathedral. I raced back to the photographer's basement darkroom and processed the film. I don't know how long I then had to wait to gain access to the enlarger upstairs. That was the photographer's sanctum sanctorum, the place where he did his alchemy and conjured his tricks of shadow and light. He allowed me to use it only when there was absolutely no likelihood he might want or need to work there.

Perhaps he'd gone out, was working in the studio, or was simply eating soup, smoking cigarettes, and drinking coffee with the old man. Anyway, I had perhaps forty-five minutes to use the enlarger. I put the first negative in the carrier and the image fell onto the easel. It was a little foggy, slightly out of focus. Or the foreground was muddy and the background too bright. I made the best print I could, and put the second negative in the enlarger.

This one was nearly identical to the first. The bishop had maintained exactly the same posture and expression while I changed the film holder and made adjustments to the camera. He looked, depending on your point of view, serious, perhaps even holy, or—as I feared—impatient. Perhaps he was glowering at the camera, at me. His small hands hung at his sides, looking not so much like they needed something to do as someplace else they wanted to be.But the point was, you could *see* all this in the second negative, or at least reasonably surmise it. It was in focus, more or less. True, the tripod had been crooked and the picture sloped off to one side and a corner of the altar was hacked off. There was also a vicious, glaring shadow falling off one of candlesticks onto the wall. And I'd positioned the camera too far off to see the bishop in detail—to frame him as the subject of the image, rather than an object within it— yet too close to incorporate the statue of St. Boniface behind him on the altar. But all in all, it was best thing I'd ever done, a near-professional quality photograph made with professional equipment and the most serious of intentions.

I had arrived, I felt, at my métier. By the first of August, I had business cards printed announcing myself "Robert H. Clark, Photographer". I got a student membership in the Professional Photographers of America. And I moved my darkroom out of my grandparents' basement and into a storage room in our apartment building. It was as dirty and inadequate as before, but it was close by, should inspiration strike.

Still, I continued to visit the photographer, to follow him around his studio and his house and, when I could, to use his darkroom. That August, the summer I was turning fourteen, you could also have found me working at his dry mounting press, putting my cathedral studies onto illustration board, building my portfolio.

I wouldn't have thought I'd become cocky or smug about my abilities or my work, but doubtless I conveyed something like that to the photographer. At that age, I carried my enthusiasms before me with manic surety. I meant well by them, but my intention—the muzzle speed at which I flung myself into the world—was heedless and overbearing. Still, the photographer treated me the same way he always had. He snaked broken-backed on his crutches through the halls in his black slacks and billowing shirts, a cigarette clenched in his mouth. I followed behind, watching his hips twist and roll.

Nothing had changed—a single summer seems a very long time when you are fourteen—and I suppose I should have been happy enough, but in some way I wanted, indeed needed, there to be a change. I wanted, I think, the photographer to see me as a photographer. But to him I was still just a kid from the neighborhood. I cannot say that he became more remote and distant, although this is how it began to seem to me. Probably I was moving away from him without knowing it. He, after all, could scarcely move at all, and rarely came out into the light of day.

One evening at the end of August, around Labor Day weekend, I was walking by the photographer's house. I'd never been there after five in the afternoon, but the sun was still up and on an impulse I went to the door and rang the bell. The customary interval—enough time to rise and right himself, seize his crutches, and begin his swaying passage to the door—passed, and he appeared. He had his cigarette and was wearing his ascot around his neck. He seemed relaxed, even jaunty. He said, pleasantly enough, "It's not a good time".

A moment later, a woman appeared in the hallway behind him. She was about my mother's age, slim and pretty. She was carrying a drink in one hand and her own cigarette in the other. She smiled at me. She wasn't wearing any shoes.

I think we acknowledged each other—I was taken aback to see anyone outside the studio in the photographer's house other than the old man—and I quickly excused myself. I felt a boundary had been crossed. I wasn't sure if it was by me having turned up unexpectedly at an unaccustomed hour, or, somehow, by him. I didn't return for several days. I'd taken to working in my own darkroom by then despite its obvious crumminess, despite the fact that everything that came out of it was in one way or another defective or spoiled.

I went back a few days later, late on a Saturday afternoon, when surely he wouldn't be working. I rang and waited, waited longer than I ever had before. I was about to leave when I saw—through the window in the door—the photographer making his way down the hall towards me slowly, as though he were moving through a fog. He opened the door unsteadily and the scent of gin eddied from his mouth. His eyes were red, dull and diffuse and unfocused. He might have been crying.

He seemed to be staring at his feet, down the sight lines of his crutches, as he spoke to me. He said, "I can't...today. I need to be alone." And with that he shut the door and turned away. I watch him shuffle and wind back down the hall. His distorted back and all its burden seemed to follow in train behind him like a snail's carapace.

I was stunned. I had never seen him like this, or in any other state than his customary quietly genial and workmanlike manner. His mood had been as smooth as his body was bent. I knew, although I could not bring the specifics into focus, that it had something to do with the woman I'd seen barefoot in her nylons a few nights before.

The photographer must have aimed to do with her what he'd done with the woman whose image filled his bedroom.

He'd pulled his twisted frame together and flung himself at a work, a beautiful and serious thing, of the same or even greater magnitude, and he'd fallen, landed pitifully, tangled in his own limbs. And I'd seen it, that great part of him that had been concealed from me, veiled in darkness until now.

I didn't go back after that. Perhaps I 'd been too shocked, or perhaps I had arrived at a point of maturity to understand that some sort of account of that evening would have to be made, and it would be less embarrassing for both of us if that moment were avoided. But in truth, I didn't want to see him again, not the way he'd been that night or even before then. I didn't want to risk seeing what he must have seen, however curious I had been about his life and history.

I began ninth grade the week after. Once, a few months later, I saw the old man out walking. He nodded at me and passed on his way. I thought that he must be pleased that things at the house had returned to the state they were in before I'd come along. I was sure he had smiled.

I didn't give up photography, not right away. I continued to use my darkroom at home, although more and more frequently it functioned as a cover for mutual masturbation with my friends and furtive cigarette smoking. I entered my cathedral photographs in a national competition sponsored by *Scholastic* magazine. The photos were returned the following spring without comment or so much as an honorable mention. But by then, I was past caring. I'd moved on. I'd outgrown tinkering with enlargers and chemicals, with lenses and exposure time and the whole apparatus of darkness and illumination.

By then I'd also drifted away from religion. I scarcely entered my own church except to please my grandparents at Christmas. I returned to the Cathedral perhaps once, that same spring, during Lent. I'd gone in for no explicable reason, and I would have been embarrassed if anyone I knew had seen me there. The Roman Catholic church had not quite entered fully into the Sister Corita felt-banner and folk mass aesthetic of the late sixties, so although the altar had been turned to face the congregation in the post Vatican II mode, other customs from the church's Gothic and Baroque past still survived.

When I entered the cathedral that day I was struck by some lack, by what I could not see, and at first I couldn't figure out what I was missing, the absence I could not grasp. Then I saw that every image in the building—every statue, painting, even the enormous crucifix over the high altar— was covered in purple cloth. The towering marble saints and apostles—bearded and fierce—that summed up the awe and intimidation I had once felt here were mute and blank, shrouded as though for burial. Their hiddenness was an immense presence.

This veiling, I learned, is imposed during the last fourteen days of Lent, and continues through Holy Week until Easter, when the cloths are removed. It's accompanied by a simplification and stripping down of ceremony, music, and even light during the mass. The services of the last three days of Holy Week are called "Tenebrae", the Latin for darkness or shadows. In the final minutes of Holy Saturday, at the beginning of the Easter midnight mass, the entire cathedral would be dark, and then one candle lit and then another until the entire building was alight, until the darkness has been driven away, every corner illuminated and revealed.

I didn't go back to the Cathedral that Easter or at any other time for some thirty years. I did sit disconsolately— watching the angel, whose beauty was never ever lost on me—with my grandparents in their Episcopal church that Easter, and at Christmas for several more years until I was old enough to opt out, to say I'd prefer not to go. I did not exactly lose my faith; rather, I put it away as in the back of the closet. I did not deny it, but merely veiled it for a stretch of time.

I suppose it was there all the while. It hadn't been destroyed or abnegated any more than those hulking statues had been during Lent. It was only hidden in the dark: you might have thrust your hand into the shadow and felt it, made out the rough shape of it with your fingers. The philosopher Hans-Georg Gadamer wrote that works of art necessarily always exist as objects but come into fullness as art only when they are being observed. Without going into their merits as sculpture, I suppose that means that during those final weeks of Lent the cathedral's veiled marble saints were still assuredly statues, but they were not quite art.

Gadamer was clarifying a point made by his teacher Heidegger that art as truth is "how self-concealing being is illuminated. Light of this kind joins its shining to and into the work. This shining, joined in the work, is the beautiful." But Gadamer takes the idea further. He wants this illumination to extend to the spectator of the artwork, to have the same self-disclosing, revelatory effect on the viewer as it does on the image he is beholding. He links it to the experience of religious awe, to the sense of the divine being, and to the possibility of redemption: "... the absolute moment in which a spectator stands is at once self-forgetfulness and reconciliation with self. That which detaches him from everything also gives him back the whole of his being."

That is art and that is God, Gadamer appears to be saying. I am as dim as I ever was back when I took up faith and a camera lens and then put them down. But now, trying to make sense of that time, feeling around in the half-light as I once did in the darkroom, it seems germane, not entirely clear but not opaque either. Let us say it is almost translucent, like the angel's stone flesh.

≈

Perhaps I'd grown tired of that light or a certain kind of illumination, of seeing things in a particular way; and what had once seemed light had turned to shadow. I had wanted, I thought, to see the unconcealed, hidden life of the photographer, but I ran away when I got a glimpse of it. I had wanted to make the beautiful still more beautiful in my photographs, but I couldn't learn to focus the lens or find the right exposure. And I wanted to be with God, but except in the form of His angel, I couldn't bear the sight of him.

Faith is supposed to be a consolation, but not a few skeptics—including myself not long after I'd worked in the darkroom for the last time—have called it a crutch. That may be, for me at least, the truth. I never bargained for faith being a burden—the labor of sustaining hope against despair, light against darkness—as it has often proved to be, and so I suppose one needs a crutch to bear it. When I was baptized I imagined it was merely beautiful, as beautiful as the lighted angel, and when it turned out be otherwise, I put it away.

Now I see it as I saw my photography, an admixture of light and dark in an unimaginable number of grays. And perhaps the living of it is a little like the photographer's life. You haul your burdens and your pain—mostly concealed—on your back and your hips, staggering forward on crutches. Sometimes, once in a long while, you make something beautiful, and it is all unveiled, transmuted into radiance.

The last time I saw the angel was at my mother's funeral, a little more than two years ago. I was looking at her, wondering if I still found her beautiful and if my judgment forty years before had been justified. I decided that I'd been right: she really was one of the few things I'd seen clearly at that time. She was beautiful, or beautiful in a particular late Victorian way, beautiful the way the Victorians idealized women as "the angel in the house" or, in the earliest photography of, say, Julia Cameron or Lewis Carroll, where girls are ethereal wraiths: pure, lovely spirit, beauty embodied, but just barely. All of it—Pre-Raphaelite annunciations, the Medievalism of Ruskin, Tennyson and Morris, and the Anglo-Catholic guardian angel in Newman and Elgar's *Dream of Gerontius*—went toward opposing the emptying out of God from the world that they saw all around them. It was a crutch.

At the funeral, people got up and, in the contemporary custom, spoke little elegies. Had I remembered, I could have recounted how, after my father had gone, my mother used to sing me a lullaby I called "Angels" because of a line in it that mentioned angels keeping watch around my bed. "Sing 'Angels'," I would plead at bedtime, and I'd keep at it until she did, until she rendered up the beautiful thing.

Now my sister was at the lectern, and I was still looking at the angel, if only for distraction. My sister was speaking about her awkward and often painful relationship with our mother; of how my mother for all her warmth and charm, was a fearful, manipulative and sometimes spiteful person. My sister was illuminating what I felt was better concealed. I might have gotten up and talked about "Angels" or offered some other picture of my mother, but I limited my own participation in the service to reading the Bible lesson. It was my role—I am the believer, the sometime churchgoer in my family—but you already see how paltry and crippled is my faith, how limited is my vision.

Not very long ago, I went down to the basement where I keep the family scrapbooks and memorabilia in order to find the wedding picture the photographer had taken of my mother. It was there, but so was another photograph I had no recollection of, a portrait of my mother taken, perhaps, for her college graduation or her engagement. The photographer had never alluded to the existence of this other photograph of my mother—he'd never acknowledged remembering photographing her at all—but there was his unmistakable signature across the bottom corner of the picture.

In this one I am not sure she is as beautiful—as goddess-like—as she in the wedding portrait. Her nose is a little too broad, her eyes a bit too small, and her expression is stern rather than happy or genial, although these were very real

features of her. She looks like someone who was capable of
anger and even vengeance. If nothing else, I think she was
trying to look serious. This was the time when she came
home from college, shorn of her faith or at least of the
Episcopal church,: the act which created the breach—
concealed to be sure—that my baptism should have
mended. And perhaps it did. We held her funeral in that
same church, and although she never expressed a preference
about the matter, I doubt she would have objected.

As I spend time looking at it, I'm more and more
inclined to think it a better photograph than the wedding
portrait. The other is perhaps more beautiful, but the
quotient of truth in this one is, for me, higher, and we are
meant to insist on the coupling of beauty and truth in art, if
only as a clichéd shorthand for what we feel we see; for the
presence we confront before which we are revealed and—
who can say?—redeemed.

Of course the photographer was not without craft here,
not without his gestures and leitmotifs, used often enough
that he might have seen them, despairing and drunk, as
gimmicks. There is, in any case, the light, and perhaps it is a
trick. It falls from above and a little to the side of her head,
and her face is numinous, veiled, but in light, a veil you can
see through. But it all comes down to the hair: it falls, the
hair and the light together, and it's nothing so much as the
hair of the stone angel. It frames my mother's face, the
radiance that's pouring out of her. I see her clearly. She's
just a few years short of bearing me, bringing me into the
world, and I'm a few more years short of asking her to sing
"Angels", begging her to sing it again and again, because I
want God the Father to protect me and because I want to be
in the presence of the song, of my mother's beautiful voice.
I'm still unbroken and uncrippled. I can walk and I can see.

4.

HOW TO LOVE

In the autumn of 1957, while my mother painted the den grey and the National Broadcasting Company, Columbia Records, and the Sisters of St. Joseph of Carondelet formed my tastes and sensibility, something happened in New York, unbeknownst to me, that would irrevocably shape my heart and desires. And since the heart's reasons, once this thing struck, became mysteries for me—imperative but beyond reason—I suppose it might even have shaped my life.

It was only a play, not even a drama, but a mere Broadway musical. It had dance numbers, choruses, love duets, conflict and swordplay, and burlesque comedy. It had, of course, a love story and, as musicals had done since "Oklahoma" a finale shadowed by a little tragedy.

It was produced by Broadway veterans and insiders: the director and choreographer had previously staged "The Pajama Game" and "Bells Are Ringing", and the music and words were respectively by the most charismatic young composer in New York and by the protégé of Broadway's master lyricist, Oscar Hammerstein. The show—for surely it was more a "show" than a "play"—was called "West Side Story".

I didn't hear anything about it for four or five years. In Minnesota we were cargo cultists: the New York culture of, say, 1957 would wash up in 1959 or '60 as flotsam from a long-spent storm. The larger world came to us through a few television and radio networks, books, and records, but there was no broad stream of national media as it's understood today. I was a child (a precocious child to be sure) only five years old when the show opened and barely nine when the movie adaption arrived. But I came to "West Side Story" by a different route.

I can't say when the Broadway cast album of the show appeared at our house. Probably my sister, five years my senior, bought it on the advice of her eighth grade classmates. I doubt it was my mother. As far as I know, none of my grown relatives, although all fans of musical theater, owned "West Side Story". It was a Broadway show, but it seemed to be the cultural property of the young.

We were very big on musicals at out house. I'd been raised on the original cast albums of "South Pacific", "My

Fair Lady", and "Carousel", the last, for all its darkness—or perhaps because of it—my favorite. Beside any of these, "West Side Story" would be considered revolutionary. But heard on the hi-fi, a show was still a show. And long after the movie soundtrack was released and became a staple in the record libraries of everyone I knew, the Broadway cast album was, as with every musical, the canonical version at our house. By the lights of our middlebrow aesthetic, Broadway shows were art but the films based on them were vulgar and false.

By "version", I'm thinking almost entirely of the recorded score. I never saw "West Side Story" performed in a theater, and I only saw the film two years after its release, when I was in the sixth grade. I was transfixed by the opening: the whistled three note leitmotif around which score was built piercing the darkness, the fields of saturated color shifting through the spectrum, the emergence of a picket row of vertical lines which become the outlines of the skyscrapers of lower Manhattan, and, finally, a silent hovering overshot that seemed to plumb the city block by block before ending in the ruins of the West Side.

Beyond that, I can't say I took unalloyed pleasure in finally seeing an actual production of the work whose music I had listened to so frequently for the previous three years. I had my prejudices towards the film medium itself; and by what right, I thought, should Maria be played by Natalie Wood, a Hollywood starlet of the grossest sort, who couldn't even sing, whose vocal performances had to be faked by the ubiquitous overdubber Marni Nixon? I hadn't seen (and couldn't have understood) Wood's performances in "Rebel Without a Cause" or "Splendor in the Grass", which she made just before playing Maria. I knew even less of who she was outside of her films: for example, that she'd met and married the love of her life, the handsome actor Robert Wagner, the same autumn that "West Side Story" had opened on Broadway; or that as she played Maria on the set of the film, that same love was disintegrating.

I was, at age eleven, a callow snob, and my tastes in musical theater were nearly as conservative as my grandparents. Bernstein's music was the whole foundation of my love for "West Side Story", but I didn't entirely care for the jazz and Latin inflections that were so central to it. I didn't like the congas, marimbas, vibes, and raunchy brass. Beyond those ethnic (as they were then called) influences, I found Bernstein's dissonances disturbing, and the blurts and blares of his horns put me on edge. That those evocations of modern life —whistles, claxons, and seething traffic—were part of the genius of the score was lost on me. Most of all, however, I think I disliked the finger-snapping that initiates "West Side Story" and which persisted as a tocsin through the entire show. It's metronome that beats in "West Side Story's" heart.

But I think my objections to the finger-snapping were less musical than visceral. It was a sound made by the kind of young men my mother called "hoods" and that the larger society called "juvenile delinquents", the menacing bongo-beat of their violence and contempt, the footfalls of older boys who would take great pleasure in beating up a kid like me.

But maybe the juicy and intimate terror it hinted at was also thrilling, those fists and their popping fingers implying not just mayhem but a kind of violation that fascinated the fatherless pre-adolescent boy that I was. Perhaps I, like my elders, feared juvenile delinquency, and perhaps I especially feared the threatening coloration it took on in "West Side Story", the amoral insouciance of cool jazz, the thrust of the mambo, the black-leather jacketed Jets, and, darker still— dark skinned—the Puerto Rican Sharks.

Bernstein had always thought that the subject of "West Side Story", much more than juvenile delinquency, was racial and religious prejudice. In 1947 Jerome Robbins had conceived the idea for an updated musical version of "Romeo and Juliet", to be set in the slums of New York. Two years later he and Leonard Bernstein began to collaborate on the project. In his copy of Shakespeare, Bernstein made a note describing the play as "an out and out plea for racial tolerance". Shortly thereafter, he and Robbins sketched out a play with the title "East Side Story" centered on a thwarted romance between a Jewish girl from the Lower East Side and an Italian Catholic boy from Greenwich Village. But the project remained stalled until 1955. In the interim, gang warfare had erupted in New York between poor Anglos and Puerto Rican immigrants. Robbins and Bernstein changed the ethnicities of the lovers and moved the locale fifty blocks north and ten blocks west. In 1957, the play opened.

"West Side Story" told no more than a love story, a love that's disparaged and then obstructed by adults, family, and social tradition: Bernardo, Maria's guardian and elder brother, insists that Maria is both too young and Tony too Anglo for their romance to be permitted. Romeo and Juliet's love was impossible because of an unnamed but ancient conflict between their families; Tony and Maria's was impossible because society—its rigid authorities and senseless prejudices—would not tolerate it and was (as I might have put it at the time) down on them, determined to quash their blameless rapture. To evade their tragedy, it would be necessary to build the better, more just, and safer world that Tony and Maria envision as they sang "somewhere...there's a place for us, a time and place for us". "West Side Story" limned the frustrations of the young, their yearnings and perennial sense of injustice, and transmuted self-pity into idealism. The pathos of youth was commensurate with the suffering of the world.

≈

I didn't fully come under the influence of "West Side Story" until I was nearly a teenager, around 1964. I was twelve and I'd danced with a girl for the very first time that autumn. And I'd also seen, however uncomprehendingly, how a tragedy in the public realm—the previous year's killing of the president, our handsome young president—could spill over into the private, the realm of lovers and families. It came to seem to me that the forces of bigotry, intolerance, and adult complacency had killed President Kennedy just as they had killed Tony and Maria.

The play did not, of course, make these connections, but it enabled me to make them myself; they felt as right and true as Bernstein's music, true as the love the music embodied. That same sense convinced me that if Barry Goldwater rather than Lyndon Johnson were elected president, we would all be incinerated in a nuclear war with the Soviets. Maybe I was a little silly to believe this, but so were millions of other Americans, a good portion of them more than twelve years old; and together, we were no sillier than Bernstein himself a few years later, clad in a Nehru jacket, entertaining the Black Panthers at his apartment on Park Avenue.

Perhaps we were all fools: young people, Midwestern naifs like me, and even the Manhattan adults situated just north of the Jets' and Sharks' old turf, who were just then becoming known as upper West Side liberals. Perhaps "West Side Story" was among the things that made us so. But surely I and others were in love: in love with lovers or our fantasies of lovers and maybe with our selves; with the images—like Tony and Maria on the fire escape balcony—of ourselves in love.

I was, to the degree I could then imagine, myself in love with that girl I had danced with, whom I had met at a dance, just as Tony and Maria had met. I remember her name was Clare, as in the order of the Sisters of the Poor Clares founded by St. Francis. I have a photo of the two of us taken there. She's brunette and a little chunky, but so am I. I am also terribly nervous. Perhaps she was not. I didn't pursue her. I didn't know where she lived or how to contact her, and in any case it wouldn't have occurred to me to seek her out: she had been given to me for an instant and then taken away.

I doubt I could have ever imagined Leonard Bernstein in love. I'd seen him on television, on the CBS "Young People's Concerts", a suavely avuncular evangelist of high culture. But of course he must have been in love, even been love-sick. Like me, he loved justice and the disadvantaged, and he loved his wife Felicia and their children with unmistakable joy and tenderness.

But he also loved and had been loved by men: his affair with Aaron Copland during his 20s was instrumental in making him a composer. When they'd parted, Copland was said to have realized that Bernstein had been the love of his life. Afterwards, Bernstein continued to love in the way he had loved Copland: he loved the men he worked with, played with, conducted with, composed with, and taught, but also, sometimes, those men he simply saw at a distance, as Tony and Maria had seen each. And his love was, I suppose, no less impossible. His heart's desire was both adulterous and antithetical to the visible fabric of the life he also loved. He loved Felicia and their children, but he also loved this other thing, this other potential life.

Bernstein was not alone. All his collaborators on "West Side Story"—the director/choreographer, the playwright, and the lyricist —were gay. They were also all Jewish, outsiders twice over. Whom and how they loved was forbidden: in 1957 you could still get arrested anywhere in America for it. So it was the most natural thing in the world for these four men to create an artwork imbued with their unnatural, impossible love, to take Shakespeare's lovers and make them not so much ill-starred as oppressed.

You might say that "West Side Story" was, in the nature of classical tragedy, ironic. But irony has today come to signify the arch and the facetious, a rueful flippancy. Perhaps it has come to this because we no longer feel comfortable with Bernstein's earnestness, his unabashed compassion, his need to attend to suffering so closely. So instead of "ironic", let us say that "West Side Story" takes Tony and Maria's situation and extends it in all directions, and especially into the realm of unsanctioned, impossible love. I suppose there is, however, one fact about "West Side Story" for which only the word "ironic" will do: that, in addition to Bernstein, Robbins, Laurents, and Sondheim, Tony, too—or rather Larry Kert, the actor that played him —was gay.

I heard nothing of all this until many years later, when, after his death, it was reported by Bernstein's biographers. As an early adolescent, I neither knew nor wanted to know much about homosexuality. Certainly I would have said, rather defensively, it had nothing to do with the mutual masturbation I sometimes practiced with my friends. That had nothing to do with attraction, never mind love.

I found my first girlfriend when I was fifteen. She was blond, pimpled, and hearty. Entangled, fully clothed, on the couch in her recreation room, I kept trying to cup her breast in my hand as we pitched and rolled. She would gently shift my hand to a less embattled locale—her hip, her sides, her flanks—and for long time I associated the feel of a female breast with the batting of a padded bra overlaid with wool or, since this was 1967, mohair.

After a Saturday night in her recreation room, I went home with a kind of flu-like ache and once in bed, frayed my penis raw. I didn't think of her while I did this. Otherwise, I took solace in entertainment, in watching my favorite TV show, "It Takes a Thief" staring Robert Wagner.

I knew that this girl wasn't the one but I also believed, as Tony had, that such a girl must be "around the corner". I also knew that when this finally happened, it would have consequences. I knew, as Tony had not known until it was too late, that someone would have pay, even to die for it.

Perhaps that sense was as much a consequence of the music as the plot: I had never seen the stage production and had seen the movie just once, but I had listened to the score at least one hundred times. The musical theme of "West Side Story", the first thing I heard the first time I played the album, was a motif of three notes: da-da-duum. It's repeated, inverted, and riffed on throughout the score: it forms the uneasy, menacing backdrop to the finger-

snapping of the Prologue but also becomes the theme of
Tony's hymn-like love song, the three notes fitted to three
syllables to his lover's name, Maria.

As the score progresses, as the love story unravels and
descends into tragedy, the motif itself dissolves. The word
"Somewhere" is sung on its first two notes, but the third
note we've grown accustomed to is withheld, a palpable
absence. By the end of "West Side Story" it has become an
echo, a single tolling note. It's the funereal bell that sounds
the tragedy of this love.

That love is an equation that can't be solved, a sentence
that can't be parsed. So within the songs that embody it,
Bernstein's music refuses to resolve itself, to reach
completion by returning to the note and key with which it
began. It's as if we've been left hanging. In a similar way,
Bernstein used appoggiatura, a leap to a dissonant note that,
in a further repetition of the chord, is replaced by the
normal note of the chord, thus "resolving" the appoggiatura.
In "West Side Story" Bernstein adapted this to produce a

kind of "bi-tonal" writing—two parallel melodies in different keys—one of which is an unresolved appoggiatura. The two voices are never allowed to mesh, to complete each other, and so the music, like the love it sings of, is disconnected, displaced, colored by the impossible.

I didn't know these terms, but I liked the music. It moved me. It was beautiful and sad. Bernstein's music entangled the beautiful and the sad together in my heart for the rest of my life. It transformed my native sentimentality, the woundedness of my childhood, into something that felt deep and eternal and otherwise ineffable, something like the transcendent, something like God.

It's said that God is love. But I couldn't tell God and Beauty and Love apart. They were all moving and sad and—despite or because of that—consoling. It's also said that there is a connection among them: some strange attraction between love and death, in "the little death" of orgasm, in the Romantic movement in poetry and music, in Wagner's "love-death" of Tristan and Isolde, and in Freud's eros and thanatos. But I didn't want to die, nor for anyone else to die. But I am not sure what I might say of martyrdom, of dying for God, for Love.

When I went head over heels for the first time, I was sixteen. The girl was a year older than me. She had a strong chin and a nervous disposition. She smoked and bit her nails. I thought she was sensitive, fragile, and artistic. I thought she needed my love to save her. I ached and burned for her. But I didn't let her know. In fact, I didn't even approach her. I would have trembled and stammered had I tried. Rather, I relied on what seemed to me an elemental law of love: that she would see me—as Tony and Maria had seen each other across the gym—and we would be irresistibly, inexorably drawn to one another. Everything else, the rest of our lives, would follow.

But she didn't notice me, or at least not in that way. A month passed and then another. I became desperate and a little angry. I imagined electrocuting myself in the school library, unscrewing a light bulb and thrusting my hand into its socket. She would see me then.

I never came close to doing this, but I pictured it many times. I sat by the communal stereo in the school gym and listened to Simon and Garfunkel's album "Bookends". She and I had been meant to board "a Greyhound in Pittsburgh", "lost" and "empty and aching", so we could look for America together.

At Christmas, I made a grand and reckless gesture. I sent her flowers, and when that produced no reaction, I sent more. Finally, in the cold and hollow days between Christmas and the New Year, she called me. She thanked me for the flowers. They were very pretty. But she hadn't understood quite why I'd sent them, why I might feel this way about her. We hadn't even dated.

Six months later, on summer vacation. I found another love. This girl was genuinely artistic: she painted and drew loopy faces in skeins of unbroken pen line. We lay down in the forest together and she took off her green army-surplus infantry jacket and her peasant blouse for me. I gazed at her breasts, their tawny nipples, and touched them too. She didn't mind, but we didn't go further. There was no need just now. Sometimes the wind came up and moved the boughs above us and we could see the sky, which she said was cerulean blue.

After the summer ended we exchanged letters. As the autumn wore on, I proposed that at Thanksgiving I should take the bus down to her town and we would rent a motel room and seal our love. She replied obliquely to this suggestion. I pressed the idea more and more in successive letters. Some time in mid-November she stopped writing back.

In the New Year I met another girl at a school dance. She followed me outside and into an empty storeroom on the school grounds. We kissed and fondled. After ten or fifteen minutes I said we ought to go back to the gym. I didn't want to seem to be coming on too strong. I tried calling her the next week. But she was always out or couldn't talk "just now". I didn't make much of this. Surely we'd made a kind of pact in that storeroom, in the dark, as Tony and Maria had made among the dressmakers dummies in the back of the store where Maria worked. I spoke to a boy who knew one of the girl's friends. He said he'd heard that the girl hadn't understood why I'd cut things short in the storeroom. Hadn't I liked her? She'd wanted to do more, maybe even to go all the way. But now she'd decided I was either a queer or simply not very interested in her. "You fucking idiot," my friend added in conclusion.

That autumn, in my freshman year of college, I finally found a requited love. Attaining it was fraught with obstacles that only made it deeper and sweeter. Among these were the fact that she lived 700 miles from me, that she was still in high school, and that she was the longstanding girlfriend of one of my closest friends. I was attending college in San Francisco and she had just moved from Minnesota to Arizona with her parents.

In November she came to California to spend Thanksgiving with her married older sister. My friend had suggested that we meet and I could show her the sights. The town in Arizona where her parents had moved was as small as it was dull. Compared to it, our home town was a metropolis, and, as for California, it was the vortex of the youth counterculture. She was prepared to be impressed.

We moved from one sight to the next, sharing and revealing ourselves, and our pilgrimage formed a succession of romantic tableaux until the city became one vast "West Side Story" gym, its hills and streets the fire escape on which our attraction ascended. By the time we went to Aquatic Park to watch the sun begin to fall over the Bay and the Marin Headlands, it seemed not only natural but ordained that we should kiss, and still more right that we should race back to my crummy rental room and take off all our clothes.

She'd had sex a few times with our mutual friend, but I was a virgin. It seemed, at first, that we didn't quite fit together, but on subsequent tries over the next hour we made it work. We would, we already knew, have to make it all work. Our love would be a struggle. So much the better, because so much more dangerous and heedless, so much more necessary the leap we had been called upon to take.

We saw each other for two more days and then she went home, to her desert tract house and her high school. We telephoned or wrote each other every day and over the next two weeks we formed a plan: we would live together in San Francisco, I eighteen, she seventeen. Everyone lived together in San Francisco without benefit of contracts and possessiveness, and everyone was young, though not perhaps as young as us.

At home in Minnesota, it was otherwise. This new way of coupling would, like "West Side Story" in the late 1950s, take several more years to reach there. Our plan was shocking even to our contemporaries. It was doubly so to our mutual friend. He'd been betrayed twice: once by her and once by me. We couldn't see the point of his anger and hurt. Our love was necessary. I came home for Christmas and one cold night near the end of the month he took me for a drive. He stopped the car next to a heap of clotted

snow and said, "I ought to beat the shit of you. But I won't".
Yes, he should have. But at the time, I would have taken it
as one more trial that proved my love's glorious
impossibility.

The adults in our lives were, of course, deeply
opposed. Curiously, it was her parents—Catholic and
working-class, her father an ex-police officer—who
acquiesced the most quickly. Provided she finished her
diploma at the high school night program I'd already located
for her in San Francisco, she could go. But she had to
promise them she would go to mass every Sunday. My
mother's objections—bohemian and liberal that she was—
were less her own than those she feared my grandparents
might have. I agreed to write them about our plan:

> *I imagine you are shocked by this and probably
> disapprove. However to us it is just as real and loving
> as any marriage. We don't find anything immoral
> about it. I hope you can believe in us.*

It was all, I suppose, about belief. My grandfather
wrote back to say that while he and my grandmother
weren't entirely comfortable with our arrangement, they

understood how times change. They would accept us as a couple. Within a few years our friends, too, were living with lovers: we'd been the avant-garde, the idealistic pioneers the blinkered world had opposed.

Our love lasted until the summer of 1972, not quite two years. After my girlfriend graduated from high school in San Francisco, we bought a Volkswagen van and moved to Mendocino County, then to Massachusetts, back to California, and finally to Los Angeles. One day, driving on Sunset Boulevard, we argued and she thrust her finger into my eye. I pulled up to the next stoplight and hit her in the face. We separated within a week. I can't remember what we had been arguing about. The reason for our love ending was as mysterious and imperative as the reason it began.

But things just as strange or marvelous were happening elsewhere in Los Angeles. A few months after our break-up, Natalie Wood and Robert Wagner remarried each other, fifteen years after their original marriage, ten years after their divorce. They had, it turned out, been made only for each other. Their particular impossible love was the only possible love after all.

I, meanwhile, was dejected and lonely. I'd found myself single, single for the first time in my post-adolescent life. In high school I'd bypassed dating in any traditional sense and then at age eighteen moved straight on to quasi-matrimony with my girlfriend. Now, at age twenty, I had to learn what my contemporaries had been working at since they were sixteen. But I'd landed in the right place. In 1972, Los Angeles rather than San Francisco might well have been called the city of love, or at least the city of sex. The west side of LA, my habitat, was crowded with single people in their twenties, drinking, meeting, and fucking. As an unattached and highly-sexed young man, it should have pleased me, should have put me squarely in hog heaven.

But my heart had its own longstanding compulsions. With anyone I actually liked (and intercourse with them inevitably made me like them even more), it seemed that love—deep, head-over-heels, monogamous love—ought to follow sex. Sex was meant to be the culmination of something, I felt; the final note of the crescendo. It wasn't clear to me if Tony and Maria ever consummated their romance. I tended to think that, yes, they must have done so after their mock wedding in the back of Maria's cousin's dress shop. If not, so much deeper the tragedy, the broken leap of their love.

Most of my contemporaries would begin to consider whether a relationship was serious after six or seven dates and weeks or even months of sex. But I didn't want a "relationship", the dispassionate passion of mutual appraisal. I wanted love, the rising appoggiatura and, if it must be, the dying fall.

Over the next three years, at least a half-dozen promising liaisons were broken off by women who could not bear my "intensity", "neediness", "coming on too strong", and "possessiveness". I was, as with my first love at sixteen, both persistent and theatrical. If a woman seemed to be uncertain or wavering in her interest, I left bouquets, letters, and small gifts on her doorstep. When these gestures failed, as they always did, it never occurred to me that they might be seen not as signs of love, but as impositions or tacit demands designed to force a particular response.

At the same time, on the other side of the country, Leonard Bernstein was pursuing a love just as intense and ill-judged. He was a family man in an almost traditional sense, and while he'd had passionate affairs with men, he'd been careful not to let these intrude on his marriage or his domestic life. But in 1973 he met an unprepossessing young man whom he soon began advertising as the love of his life.

Bernstein became almost willfully indiscreet. He had liaisons with his new love at the family apartment on Central Park West, culminating in Felicia discovering him and the young man in bed together. She issued an ultimatum and Bernstein moved out. He lived with his lover on Central Park South for not quite two years. He was "out" at last. He and his lover combed anthologies for poem with gay themes that Bernstein might set for a song cycle. But his heart was not in it. In 1977 he and Felicia reconciled and Bernstein returned home.

That same year, now restored to his wife and children and the family life he loved, he did manage to compose one song: a jaggedly tender setting of Whitman's "To What You Said", a succession of unresolved appoggiaturas that reflected the poem's resigned celebration of love between men:

> To what you said, passionately clasping my hand, this is
> my answer:
> Though you have strayed hither, for my sake, you can
> never belong to me, nor I to you...
> Behold love choked, correct, polite, always suspicious
> Behold the received models of the parlors—What are they
> to me?
> What to these young men that travel with me?

Bernstein's setting of the poem was one of the loveliest and the most haunting things he ever wrote, perhaps the last great thing he wrote, an elegy to impossible love. But even what seemed possible—comfortable, familial, and longstanding—could not last. A few months after they reconciled, Felicia was diagnosed with cancer and by the following June she was dead.

≈

I don't recollect being aware of Felicia's death. But there was another tragedy three years later I could not escape. Natalie Wood, aged forty-three, died on November 29, 1981. She fell from the deck of Robert Wagner's yacht "Splendour" and drowned. There were alcohol and drugs in her blood. She'd been having a love affair with her co-star in a new movie. I had by that time changed my opinion

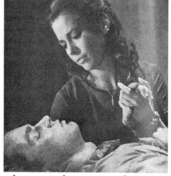

about her. Her beauty, her pure but spunky manner, seemed a kind of transcendent good. She was Maria. I would have married her in an instant. I already loved her. I believed Wagner had had a hand in her death or had let her drown.

Meanwhile, myself in a nimbus of cocaine, I'd fallen in love once more. My beloved was the best friend of my best friend's girlfriend. Our relationship was both symmetrical and synergistic, parallel friendships intersecting in adjacent love affairs. The passion was effortless, a haven of ease after all my mischance as a single. But perhaps that, too, was a kind of impossible love: passion, after all, is high emotion, even suffering. But I was tired of struggle. I wanted to lay down my arms.

I had at last gotten everything I thought I wanted and I'd scarcely had to ask. We moved in together after a week and we got married not many months later. It was easy and I was placid, and it seemed to me that this love was a

mature love, the kind of relationship you could count on for
the long haul, that you could settle down in, happily settle
for.

That might have been what I thought I wanted, but it
was not my heart's desire. I kept pressing the marriage to
the edge. I moved us around from house to house, even
from country to country. I switched my putative career a
half-dozen times. I drank too much. My demeanor
ricocheted between tetchiness and bonhomie. It was as
though in order to keep the love alive, it had to be forever
in forward motion, not just steadily moving but aloft on the
rising action of a drama. And if circumstances could not
supply that drama, I would supply it myself. My wife,
impassive, standing still, endured.

The marriage died in 1990, the same year as Leonard
Bernstein. The last two major recordings he'd completed
were an operatic treatment of "West Side Story" and then,
in the final months of his life, a concert version of
"Candide". I spent that summer listening to "Candide" while
I waited for my separation to be formalized and painted the
house I had built to save our marriage. It would need be
sold, at a loss as it turned out, as these things must go. As I
painted, the trials and betrayals of Candide played over and
over again. The petro-chemical stink of oil paint hung in my
mouth like—as one of the show's laments put it—
wormwood and gall.

"Candide" was both the predecessor and antithesis of
"West Side Story". Bernstein composed it just before "West
Side Story" and even recycled unused material from it into
the later show. It's a worldly-wise, even cynical tale that
equates romantic love with either willful folly or a
contemptuous optimism that dismisses suffering as someone
else's problem. But in the end, the play is not entirely
jaded. Love may be a dangerous sham, but something like
love—reformed along rational, disillusioned lines—can

perhaps be put in its place. "Candide" posits a possible love, but Bernstein, like me, craved its impossible counterpart. "Candide", then, was the threshold of "West Side Story", the cliff from which Tony and Maria would throw themselves.

I found another love. She was thirteen years my junior, lived in a distant city, and was strikingly different from me in temperament. She was pretty, idealistic, and spunky. She was, I suppose, unattainable, as—still being married—was I. Accordingly, I staked everything on our love. I threw myself at her, at the new life I fancied we would make together out of ourselves and nothing more.

She liked me well enough and even admitted she'd been attracted to me. But she couldn't quite comprehend the depth of the feeling I had for her. What, she seemed to ask, did it have to do with anything—with my circumstances or hers, with my divorce or the future of my child or the career she was just then establishing for herself? She did not so much accept or reject me as shake her head, mystified.

I decided to withdraw until my divorce came through, until the time when there would be no barriers between us. I wrote her a letter. I said I would keep my distance, however much it would hurt. It was one more sacrifice I was willing to make for this love, to put it away and live alone in the dark without it.

Six months went by. They passed like a hard winter, snowless but frigid, and I might have been living in a cave. But I would stick it out. My divorce would be behind me and then she would see how it should be between us, just as my first love at sixteen was meant to see it: among the roses, the Greyhound bus bound for "America", the boy's corpse on the library floor.

She called me one night. She made no reference to the fact that we hadn't spoken for months, or that, to my mind, we had made a kind of pact to avert our eyes from another.

She was jocular but there was a strain in her voice, a trace of fluster. Did I remember the migraines she'd had, that she'd told me about, a year or more ago, when we were still talking? Of course I did. I remembered all the things she'd ever told me about herself, venerated and worried over each little fragment, blew on them like guttering coals during my exile.

Well, she had a brain tumor. Wasn't that strange, the very last thing you might think of when you were scarcely twenty-eight years old? The joke was on her, she seemed to say. Funny old world. She was smart and wry and resigned and terrified, a little like Natalie Wood in "Inside Daisy Clover". I said I would come down and see her the next day. She said that would be good.

So we were going to be reunited for reasons I could never have foreseen. I drove the two hundred miles, half in dread, half in yearning. When I arrived at her apartment she was more composed than she'd been the previous night. She admitted her prognosis was good. She would have to undergo neurosurgery of an invasive, serious, but not overly hazardous kind.

We talked for the rest of the afternoon and had dinner that night. She was optimistic, and listening to her, I became optimistic. Perhaps the months apart, in exile, had been worth it in order to arrive at this moment. She seemed to accept me—my worry and care—completely: she wasn't pushing me away, she wasn't puzzling out what sort of sense we made together.

But she was thinking about her future, the mere possibility of her surviving, while I was thinking about *our* future, about the possibility of she and I being together when the nightmare was over. As the evening continued, she told me what else had transpired in her life in the months since we'd last talked. She'd met someone she really liked. Earlier that afternoon in her apartment, I'd noticed two toothbrushes hanging in her bathroom. Now I knew whom the second one belonged to.

I felt horror and then shame, realizing the horror was ignoble under the circumstances, that I should scarcely care whom she might decide to share her life with when she soon might have no life at all. Then, for a long time, I felt nauseous and hollow. We kept talking and I tried to be convivial and encouraging.

At home, I resolved to be noble, to take my suffering and transmute it into something that might aid her in her own. But ultimately, she no more wanted that sacrifice than the earlier one I'd tried to make her accept—that of my old life as husband and father. I pressed her. There was nothing I would not do. Her surgery was going to be performed on the other side of the country where a neurosurgeon experienced in the procedure had his practice. I bought a plane ticket to be there, and over the course of several weeks of telephone conversations she told me she'd prefer I didn't come east to the hospital; that she really didn't want anyone there but her parents. I wondered if this was because she wanted her new lover there instead.

The day she had the surgery, I called the hospital every few hours and persuaded a nurse that I was a close relative. But the account I got wasn't what I'd been told to expect. Yes, she had been in surgery, gone to the recovery room, and been sent back to her bed. But then she'd gone back for a further operation, and then a third. After forty-eight hours, I got more information. Her brain had been bleeding since the first surgery and successive procedures had failed to stop it. I knew, when I called the next day, that she would be dead. And so she was.

I went to the funeral and wept. Her family was kind to me. She had liked me so much, they said. She thought so highly of me. No one there knew, nor could I allow myself to say, what I had felt about her, what I had envisioned for us. I finally saw and then met her lover there. He was shattered and genial. A few weeks before the surgery she had said to me, "You and I are so much alike". As with everything she said, I interpreted this in the light of my hope for our love: that being alike, we were meant to be together. But her lover was nothing like me at all.

For the next year, I carried all this with me like a relic, both talisman and stain. A drama had befallen me that was neither comedy nor tragedy. My lover and I had not lived happily ever after. Nor did death steal her away just at the moment when we were at last united. As far as the world knew, I had simply lost a friend. That was sad, but it was not tragedy. It was not Tony and Maria. But for me, it seemed that because I would have suffered the tragedy, if only given the chance, I was as good as being the tragedy's victim.

It had been my life, my great work—this impossible love—for more than a year. I'd suffered for it and sacrificed for it. I'd bet everything upon it and put myself head-on in the path of grief in order to pursue it. It seemed to me that something ought to have come out of all that, something profound. But it refused to mean anything, to be more than happenstance. I had, unlike Tony, unlike the woman I believed I had loved, merely gotten away with my life.

Leonard Bernstein, I believe, could never escape the power of the things he'd created. The dilemmas and feelings he might have imagined mastering through artistic expression only continued to master him. After composing "To What You Said", in the early 1980s he envisioned a larger project, a full-scale opera, called "A Quiet Place"

which was to be his masterwork. It was to be the story of a family with a bisexual husband at its center.

"A Quiet Place" received middling to scathing reviews and was cited as evidence of Bernstein's decline as a composer. Rather more kindly, his "West Side Story" collaborator Stephen Sondheim suggested that perhaps Bernstein had become afflicted with what he called "importantitis", a proclivity for grand statement that tended towards pretension and sentimentality. Or perhaps he failed to realize that his own impossible love could not be explicated or even expressed in music and drama . He could only flail against and around the unsayable enigma of it. It was beyond the capacity of art, at least his art, to give it voice. So he gave up composing and went back to conducting and recording, and, at the very last, to "West Side Story" and finally "Candide".

He died of something like exhaustion. He was a heavy— one might say almost passionate—smoker of cigarettes, which took a toll on his lungs and heart. But it was conducting that killed him. He took on more engagements than his body could cope with, spread across the world in Vienna, Israel, Japan, and New York. And of course when the Berlin Wall fell, he needed to be there, to conduct Beethoven. That was perhaps his conceit, his sense of himself as a global star. But who was more suited to lead a reunited Berlin in "Ode to Joy" than this exuberant, gray-maned, and not incidentally Jewish virtuoso of possibility?

Bernstein spent his final months recording "Candide" in London, worrying his family and friends in New York, and ushering in a new era of peace in once divided Europe. Or so he might have wished. It seems naive now. The world cannot be healed by love and mere good will or, as the collapse of Marxism showed, human devisings. Bernstein's conception of art claimed the gift of prophecy. But it was "Candide" rather than "West Side Story" that was prophetic. Death is unconquerable, and least of all by love. Ask Natalie or Felicia or my beautiful young friend. Ask Tony and Maria.

As I wrote this, a new Bernstein recording was released, an obscure work from the period just before "Candide". It's "Peter Pan", and its two most deeply felt songs are "Who Am I?" and "Build My House". Perhaps "Peter Pan"—boyhood, both tender and heroic, impossibly attenuated—rather than "Candide" or even "West Side Story" is Bernstein's key work. Maybe his—and, I can't help but think, my own— devotion to art, idealism, and Eros were the outer garb of a unstanchable immaturity, a clutching at the consolations and terrors of childhood.

And perhaps the true cause of tragedy—the necessary fault—is naiveté or, if you like, hope and faith, the wish for love, God's or that of another human body. But I don't understand quite what to put in their place. The alternatives look dull and shabby. I still want to say, along with Whitman and Bernstein, "Behold love choked, correct, polite, always suspicious/Behold the received models of the parlors—What are they to me?". And I am still stupidly convinced that art can bring you to the threshold of salvation, if not the means to seize it.

It was art, it was "West Side Story" that taught me the way I wanted love to feel, that drove me to seek that feeling again and again, that initiated me into mysteries that still remain veiled. It schooled me in foolish hope and misplaced faith, in heedless belief and headlong desire. It taught me, for better or worse but altogether irresistibly, how to love. I was and am incorrigible, past reform, impossible.

Later, I found love again. My lover—two years later, my wife—and I saw each other across a crowded distance in a club, and I felt compelled to go to her. Two years after we met, we had a son. I was still anxious, intense and fanciful, but she had a head on her shoulders. She had no use for musicals. That's not to say she was only practical: she was also very pretty. People said that she looked a little like Natalie Wood

What we made together seemed for a long time to be less a state of feeling—of passion, say, or rapture—than a place. Ever since I was a boy, at least from 1957, the autumn of the premiere of "West Side Story", I have felt displaced. I craved the "Somewhere" that Tony and Maria sought and never found. I believed I could arrive at it only through love and art, impossible love and unattainable beauty.

But then, with my wife, I was settled just *here*, rooted among real and palpable persons, none of them ideal, myself least of all. It wasn't the timorous, resigned garden proposed at the end of "Candide". Rather, it was merely home. It contained solace, peace, and sometimes joy, but also boredom, despair and anger. Most of the time I liked it well enough, but since I came there by a different path than I imagined, I needed a fair amount of reassurance that that place was really beautiful, that it was the proximate heaven it sometimes seemed. It was not how I had pictured things. So I needed to be sure, to be told almost every day, that that place was indeed somewhere after all.

As it turned out, she and I were not in a place, but a time whose length could be measured in seventeen years. Then our time was over and a new time began. We'd seen one another and walked a long ways together and then we parted, although it was some time before I noticed she was gone. Like every time, once recollected, I suppose it will become the object of hollowed-out longing, of nostalgic regret, and finally sentimentality as I begin to misremember it. I do not blame her or even myself, and perhaps in this alone I have gained a little wisdom. I blame God, who has woven suffering so inextricably into love, whose love, the lives of saints tell me, is the greatest suffering of all.

As for romance, I don't think I have so much lowered my expectations as shifted them. I used to think God was love or, really, that Love was god, or that love—the feeling of it—was the ultimate transcendent, the source of life, not simply the expression of it. Without it you were good as dead. No wonder I brought such desperate urgency to every relationship. And no wonder those loves did not work out. No one can be or wants to be another person's God. It's more than any person can bear. It's impossible.

Yet sometimes you see another person across the distance, among the dancers in the gym; and it's true, despite your feeling, that they are only a person. But it's also true that what you see is, unmistakably, always and everywhere, heaven.

5.

SCOTT & BEN

I first read *The Great Gatsby* in a sophomore high school English class, the only course at St. Paul Academy that interested me. The school advertised itself as a "Country Day School" which, located in the center of our city, it scarcely seemed to me to be; but more chiefly it claimed to be a "college preparatory school", which it certainly was. Its sole mission was to ship its graduates off to Ivy League or at least eastern colleges. As early as the fourth grade I was warned that if I didn't start studying harder then and there, I wouldn't get accepted eight years later at "a good school" and this, I was given to understand, would be a kind of ultimate and irrevocable failure.

My father, Thomas Clark, attended St. Paul Academy, and so had my grandfather, Benjamin Griggs, and so, I vaguely knew, had F. Scott Fitzgerald. The school made little of this fact when it made anything of it all: lore held that Fitzgerald had stayed until 1912, his own sophomore year, when he went east to be "prepped" at a boarding school. St. Paul Academy at that time lacked the luster to guarantee admission at, say, Princeton, where Fitzgerald later matriculated. (My grandfather, a grade below him, followed the same path east and finished up at Yale).

It was known that while at St. Paul Academy, Fitzgerald had contributed some journeyman fiction and drama pieces to the school paper, called *Now and Then*. I can't recall any of these ever having been displayed, read, or their existence in any way noted. In fact, the only mention of Fitzgerald I can remember being made at our school was a comment about him from a 1910 issue of *Now and Then,* which said, "If anybody can poison Scotty or stop his mouth in some way, the school at large and myself will be obliged". The remark was at Fitzgerald's expense, implying that the school had wanted to bring "Scotty" down a peg, and also that in 1967, by repeating it, the school still did. That, and the silence otherwise accorded his one-time presence there, suggested that as far as Saint Paul Academy was concerned, Fitzgerald was a failure, even if he had gotten into Princeton.

It seemed, then, that *The Great Gatsby* we read in English class might have been written by someone else entirely, some other F. Scott Fitzgerald who held no relation to this largely unnoted alumnus of our school. The book's selection arose from its place in the larger realm of literature, of Shakespeare and Yeats, and of Hemingway's *The Old Man and the Sea* and Hershey's *Hiroshima*, which we also read that year. I can't say that these others didn't make an impression, but I think Fitzgerald ultimately touched us

more deeply, or at least me, who passed my time at St. Paul
Academy in a state of aching boredom and resentment.

Maybe the teacher understood that *Gatsby* was a young
person's book, if only in the way it so embodied an
adolescent vision of a life the young might hope to have
after high school and college: that yearning for wealth,
success, and glamour alloyed to a stunningly innocent faith
in the goodness of beauty, and of the beauty and goodness
of the opposite sex. And for my schoolmates and me, its
power was doubled by also being a story of Midwesterners
trying their luck in the East, the log of a voyage out from
and back to St. Paul, even if in our reading of *Gatsby* we
evaded the question of whether returning home was a kind
of defeat.

In 1990, although I'd managed to stay away from St.
Paul for the better part of twenty years, I came back for a
little while. It was the last time I saw my grandfather. His
mind had grown clouded in recent years, or at least he'd
become a little abstracted, and I was looking for a subject
that might engage him. I'd gathered from my mother that
he'd actually known Fitzgerald slightly in their time at St.
Paul's, and so I asked him about Fitzgerald.

He and my grandmother were sitting in their bedroom
in their St. Paul apartment, she tucked into her twin bed
watching a daytime game show on the television, he sitting
on a chair next to her. My grandfather had always seemed a
reticent, unforthcoming, and even forbidding figure, and I
supposed—not without reason—that he saw me as an
aimless, self-involved young man of no commendable
prospects. He was wearing a bathrobe—of flannel, in a
shade of oxblood, or so I want to say. I asked him
something like, "Tell me about F. Scott Fitzgerald," and,
after a moment, he exhaled and looked up at me. Then he
looked back down, as though at his hands resting in his lap,
and began to shake his head from side to side in broad arcs. I

thought at first this indicated a kind of wistfulness, of recollecting a time that was very long ago when they had all been young and foolish but innocent. I am sure it contained that, but he continued to shake his head, perhaps just a moment longer, and then the gesture took on the character of a deep and widening regret, grief, or even anger. He stopped and looked up at me again and I am sure he said, "What a waste". But I do not really know if he had even opened his mouth, or if I had merely read it in the shaking of his head.

I could see he had nothing more to say about it, and I changed the subject to baseball or, more pointlessly, about whether he would get up to his house on Lake Superior this summer. We both knew, of course, that he would not. He was dead within a year.

Some months later, I reread *The Great Gatsby*, and I also read *This Side of Paradise*, *The Beautiful and the Damned*, and *Tender is the Night* for the first time. This was not my idea, but my wife's. She loved these books, she thought I would love them too, and perhaps she felt they contained something I needed. So I read them. Shortly after that I wrote my own first novel. Then I began to try to answer the question I had put to my grandfather or, perhaps more exactly, to read the forlorn and tender motion he had made in response.

F. Scott Fitzgerald died on December 21, 1940. I don't know if much was of made it in St. Paul or at my grandfather's home. It was Christmastime. My mother was putting in her college application to Vassar, where Fitzgerald's daughter Scottie had matriculated a year earlier. Certainly no one was surprised by his death, even if

he was scarcely forty-four years old: it, sooner rather than
later, was inevitable. It was not the culmination or
apotheosis of anything. In *Tender is the* Night, he'd written:

> Dick Diver doesn't want to be just one of
> these clever boys. He must be destroyed a
> little, he must be less intact. And if life won't
> do it for him, it's no substitute to go out and
> get himself a disease or a broken heart or an
> inferiority complex.

Dick is an alcoholic but he's also a kind of Romantic
saint, a martyr. He has to annihilate himself to achieve his
great work. Fitzgerald had to do the same thing. The writer
doesn't shape his material: it shapes him. He submits to it
and is subsumed within it, even unto death. While
composing *Tender is the Night*, Scott was also reading
Oswald Spengler's *The Decline of the West*, which argued that
civilizations and their history are not progressive but
entropic; they flourish and then fizzle and die out. And
since his mid-twenties, the age when he was writing *Gatsby*,
Fitzgerald had been a connoisseur of old love. He had an
uncanny sense of the sentimentality people developed about
their historical selves, especially the young self, and the
pangs of memory that sustain and enlarge it. It's a highly
refined sort of self-consciousness, a fashioning of legends
about one's own life, as if to say, just then, for that
moment, one's life *signified*.

I can't say that my grandfather ever read *Tender is the
Night* or even *The Great Gatsby*. I know his library did
contain *This Side of Paradise*, which was written in St. Paul
after Fitzgerald's discharge from the military, and *The*

Beautiful and the Damned, which was published during Scott's last stay there in 1922. I discovered this and a little more the summer after he died. I went to help clear out his house on Lake Superior. Its contents were not of much interest to his other relatives and I came away with a carload of photographs and slides, scrapbooks, and bric-a-brac.

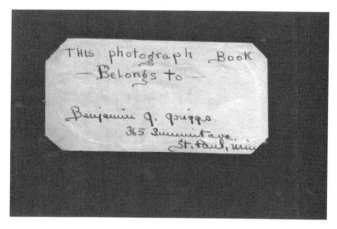

Over the next several years, I delved. I studied my grandfather's relics, not so much to understand him as to keep his presence within reach, to prevent it from sinking irretrievably into the past. It seemed to me that somehow the point of my own life was somehow tied to the persistence of his, that without it I would become unmoored. At the same time, I was reading Fitzgerald and then one and then another biography of him. I needed Scott too, as a talisman, if not as a mentor or model. You wouldn't want to emulate his life, and as for his art, I had no illusions about my talent. But it seemed to me very important that someone from the same world as me, right down to the same school and the same neighborhood, could be a writer, and a writer of genius.

Then, in a Fitzgerald biography, I came across my grandfather's name, Ben Griggs. He and Scott Fitzgerald had played together, known each other as boys. They'd gone to dancing classes together, roughhoused in the vacant lot next to the Griggs family home on Summit Avenue, played detective, Indians, and explorers in the alleys and lanes behind it, and admired and played kissing games with the same girls. My grandfather had never mentioned any of this.

Of course, he never spoke of even reading Fitzgerald. And perhaps he didn't need to. He'd lived in the same collegiate milieu Fitzgerald described in *This Side of Paradise*, and he was acquainted with the orgiastic consumption of bootleg liquor recorded in *The Beautiful and the Damned*. He was, like most of his generation (or at least the swatch of it to which he belonged), a formidable drinker. That, too, had been part of the upper middle class, collegiate portfolio of the "Yale man" he became. So when he won a squash championship, a characteristic display of his athleticism, the trophy he received was an engraved silver cocktail shaker. This was at the apex of prohibition, when merely to fill the shaker was a violation of federal law. It was among the things I took away from his house, and I have it now in my own kitchen. It's dented and the silver plate is mottled with brownish-orange patches like liver spots that no amount of polish will remove. It's seen much use, sloughed off several skins, and now it's retired, under my care, eighty-five years on.

After seeing my grandfather's name in the Fitzgerald biography, I asked my mother more about their connection, and the first thing that came to her mind was related to drinking. She said that when Scott returned with Zelda to live in St. Paul for a year in 1921 and '22, they'd gone for a bobsled ride with my grandfather and grandmother. Zelda was so drunk she'd fallen off the sled, not once but several times, and she had pulled others off with her. My grandmother, a formidable debutante from Philadelphia and

just then affianced to my grandfather, was not amused by
this, and there was not much further contact—so my
mother said—between the Fitzgeralds and the Griggs.

To me, this story had the whiff of the apocryphal about
it, of well known facts about the protagonists—in this case,
their drinking—embroidered onto an archetypal Minnesota
winter scene. But there in the December 1921 entry in
Scott's ledger—his month-by-month record of his life—is
the phrase "bob rides". That this likely relates to
humiliations or untoward incidents during these rides is
almost certain, for Scott's ledger tended to highlight not his
successes or fond memories but his failures: the
embarrassments, broken friendships, and evictions that
increasingly characterized his life in those years, and which
in 1924 and '26 attained such a quantity that Scott was
moved to compose a separate "Snub List" of people who had
dropped him or given him the cold shoulder.

So it's not unsurprising that my grandparents might
have been among this number, however amenable they
were to fun and boozing. The rest of St. Paul had done
pretty much the same, and so the Fitzgeralds soon left for
the east, for New York, Long Island, and Europe, to the

denouement of their lives. My grandfather never saw either
of them again. The one photograph he possessed of Scott

shows him at Dellwood, holding forth, gesticulating towards an audience oblivious to him. He seems, as he would put it himself, "a bit tight."

For all that, something came out of that year in St. Paul, or at least something was laid to rest. It had been Scott's second homecoming in as many years. The first time, in 1919, he'd come back a relative failure, having left Princeton without graduating, served in the military without seeing action, and suffered the rejection of his first novel. My grandfather, I later learned, set him up with a job at the Griggs wholesale grocery business, but at the last minute Scott turned it down. Instead, he shuttered himself in his parent's home and revised his novel once more. It was published a year later as *This Side of Paradise*. And with that, the next time he returned to St. Paul, in 1921, he was a success, even a celebrity, for all the good that did him.

Every morning on my way to school, I used to walk by the house where Scott finished that first novel. There was a vicious dog in the next block, and my paternal grandparents lived just down and across the street in one of the ugliest homes to grace Summit Avenue. Directly across from the Fitzgerald house, visible from the room where Scott wrote the book that launched his career, there was a vacant lot, and it was here that I got drunk for the first time, on peppermint schnapps, aged 16. I am pretty sure that I passed out briefly in the snow that night, and I suppose I might have frozen to death. These things have happened in St. Paul, even to boys like me.

Initially, Scott made a positive impression on his second homecoming, and he did not overplay the triumphant author. He organized amateur dramatics and produced a satirical newspaper for the University Club in which he featured himself, my grandfather, and all their cohort. In one issue, a Griggs relation is described as having been delegated to lead the cotillion but "unfortunately arrived in no condition to lead anything". In another, my grandfather is pictured in a mock fashion lay-out wearing plus-fours:

EVERY PICTURE TELLS A STORY

Miss Betty Griggs, at the left, is so enamored of her Gordon Sports Jacket she just can't help hugging it. Mr. B. G. Griggs is demonstrating how a G. S. J. accentuates the slender boyish figure so fashionable these days. It's not so easy to psychoanalyze Mr. George Smith, our state professional champion—perhaps he's thinking that, armored with a Gordon Jacket he can't lose, or now that he has one, that losing or winning is of small importance—who knows! At the right Mrs. Walter Kennedy has just made a 666 yard drive straight down the fairway, due entirely—almost entirely—to the fact she is confident she looks her smartest in that Gordon Sports Coat. That golfer hiding behind the tree in the background is so ashamed—his papa wouldn't buy him a G. S. J.—It's a grand picture.

slender, leaning insouciantly against a golf club, a cigarette between his fingers, his hair parted down the middle, just like Scott's.

But then followed the sleigh rides, and then he and Zelda moved for the summer to the White Bear Yacht Club in Dellwood. During Scott's childhood the St. Paul elite kept their summer "cottages" (in truth, quite substantial houses) here, but in 1921, with the advent of the automobile, Dellwood was becoming an upper-crust suburb. By the time I was a boy that transformation was complete. As a teenager, I was invited to a St. Paul Academy party at a large house on the lake. It was on that night that I first experienced the inchoate yet clear sensation of being somewhere I didn't belong. There was wealth, of course, and a kind of effortless confidence that seemed to go with it. At the turn of the century my great-grandparents themselves had a "cottage" here, but in the intervening sixty years the fortunes of my family had subsided to the upper tiers of the middle class.

The kids from Dellwood were nice enough: they condescended to me in the antique, gracious sense of the word. But something in the atmosphere—the breeze off the lake, the quickening stars at dusk—made me talk too much or clam up at inopportune times or say the wrong things. There was a girl, pretty and easily amused, born of and for this place, and she drew me toward her. But before I spoke, before she even looked back at me, I saw and knew that she was meant for other things and persons than me, consecrated to a vocation beyond anything I might attain. Had I the talent, I might have written, "Her body hovered delicately on the last edge of childhood, she was almost eighteen, nearly complete, but the dew was still on her." She might have been out of reach, but I could have made an image of her with such words.

At Dellwood, Scott and Zelda's drinking and rowdiness became more than St. Paul could bear. After repeated complaints and warnings, he and Zelda were told to leave the club. They moved to the Commodore Hotel for six weeks and then they left St. Paul for New York. Scott never went back, although he kept up a correspondence with

Elizabeth Ames Jackson, his closest female childhood friend

there, a role she also played for my grandfather. She and my grandfather had been in France together at the same time during World War I, she a nurse's aide, Ben an ambulance driver. I was brought up calling her "Aunt Betty".

So Scott had lost St. Paul, perhaps as he needed to or intended to. But what he took away was *The Great Gatsby*, or at least the vital germ of it. It's generally assumed *Gatsby* was based on Scott and Zelda's residence in Westport, Connecticut, before their move to St. Paul, and in Great Neck, Long Island, immediately afterward—spun from events and personalities then current in the world of New York bootleggers and stock speculators. But those elements were less the core of the novel than its superstructure. Fitzgerald took its heart—its preoccupations and raison d'être—away with him from White Bear Lake. During his last few weeks in St. Paul, Scott wrote a short story called "Winter Dreams". It's about a working-class boy named Dexter who grows up among the swells who summer at a resort called Black Bear Lake. He works as a caddy and at age fourteen, he encounters a spoiled and pretty rich girl on the cusp of adolescence.

Dexter gives her no further thought and scrimps and saves to attend an eastern college. After graduation he returns to open a successful chain of steam laundries and, at age twenty-three, finds himself back on the golf course where he once caddied, playing a round with the wealthy men whose clubs he used to carry. They don't remember him in that role, but as he walks the course, he has "the sense of being a trespasser" and "found himself glancing at the four caddies who trailed them, trying to catch a gleam or gesture that would remind him of himself, that would lessen the gap that lay between his present and his past".

What he does rediscover is the girl, still lovely and spoiled, now a bored, coquettish twenty-year-old. Over the next two years they have a cat-and-mouse courtship.

Finally, just as Dexter on the verge of marrying another girl, she offers herself. Dexter breaks his engagement, and is, of course, then dropped by the girl. She's not, and never has been, meant for him.

Seven years a later, a client brings him news of the beautiful girl: she's living in Detroit, married to a man who drinks too much and abuses her. And, the client adds, she's no longer beautiful.

> Something had been taken from him... gingham on the golf-links and the dry sun and the gold color of her neck's soft down...Why, these things were no longer in the world! They had existed and existed no longer. Even the grief he could have borne was left behind in the country of illusion, of youth, of the richness of life, where his winter dreams had flourished.

It's all here, the parts that mattered, the cruel and tender logic of *Gatsby*: "So we beat on, boats against the current, borne back ceaselessly into the past"; the fact that time and youth are not a progress but a regress from adulthood back towards childhood, from the east back to the Midwest, from hope to regret. It's all he needed for the rest of his life and the rest of his work.

I spent ten years, as much time as Scott spent writing *Tender is the Night*, excavating the pasts of my grandfather and of F. Scott Fitzgerald. I don't think it was ever a morbid obsession, but it hovered over everything I did.

I became a Roman Catholic, the religion of Scott's youth, although I am as sure as I can be that he had nothing to do with it. I often wondered why there so little trace of his religion in his work; why, as far as I could see, the "Catholic element" he had once promised Max Perkins would factor in *Gatsby* was nowhere in evidence in the finished book. After my conversion, I wrote a family memoir called *My Grandfather's House*, and perhaps, as far as the past went, I should have stopped there. I couldn't: I went full bore at Fitzgerald and his circle. I wrote a book proposal for a group biography of Fitzgerald, Ernest Hemingway, and John Dos Passos which two dozen New York publishers could not see any point in. It was both old hat and, I suspect, grandiose. But I couldn't let the research go to waste, and in fact I did more research, as though I couldn't stop myself. After a further year I wrote a ninety-five-page essay on Fitzgerald's life during the composition of *Tender is the Night*. What I'd created was both too long to be published as an essay and too short to be a book. I sent it out to journals and publishers. The rejections were apologetic and kind—the essay was "beautifully written" and obviously reflected a great deal of labor—but it seemed as though I were being congratulated for accumulating a particularly fine collection of stamps or baseball cards.

I put that project aside long enough to write a novel about writers and artists living in Europe; about the dangers of pursuing beauty and art too intently. It, too, was rejected by a score of major publishers, among them Scott's old house, Scribners. Around that time I became depressed and bitter. I drank too much and my marriage and friendships began to fray. I took medication and tried to give up writing.

Things began to go a little better—they often do despite Spengler's sureties. I got a grant to write a non-fiction book and I began to write essays. And I took out my boxes of Scott Fitzgerald and Ben Griggs memorabilia once more: the family scrapbooks, letters, and photos but also the Xeroxes I'd taken away from hours of digging in the

Fitzgerald archive at Princeton. And at the very end of it, by way of a rare book dealer, I finally read Scott's student contributions to the St. Paul Academy *Now and Then*.

Excluding some short poems and drama, these amounted to four pieces, and the fact that they had later gone utterly unremarked at St. Paul Academy spoke, for me, in their favor. My own experience there suggested that the school was willfully indifferent to art, imagination, or any kind of non-conformity. Scott's *Now and Then* juvenilia might be—must be, I couldn't help but think—possessed of his genius; might, in fact, contain its seed, its secret.

But reading them, despite my hopes, I had to confess that even as specimens of precocity, the pieces were at best tiresome exercises. One was a clumsy mystery and another a football tale, "Reade, Substitute Half," in which a heretofore mediocrity on the team saves the day.

But there was something more in the last story, "A Debt of Honor". On its face, it wasn't much more than "Reade, Substitute Half" transposed to the Civil War. Private Jack Sanderson of the Confederate Army is court-martialed for falling asleep on sentry duty, an offense serious enough to warrant the firing squad. But General Robert E. Lee himself intervenes, commuting Sanderson's sentence "on account of your extreme youth". Six weeks later, at Chancellorsville, he single-handedly charges a Union infantry emplacement and sends its defenders fleeing. Later that day searchers find "the body of him who had once been John Sanderson, Third Virginia. He had paid his debt".

I liked those closing phrases, the melancholy irony of "him who had once been John Sanderson," the final tolling of "Third Virginia," and the fact of Sanderson sacrificing himself for what will be, after all, the losing side. I suppose, however, that, when all is said and done, it's pat in the manner of most high-minded tributes to duty and sacrifice: it substitutes sentiment for genuine tragedy.

But Scott was thirteen years old when he wrote this. He was, I felt, entitled to view death as an ennobling abstraction. At the same time, I couldn't help but feel he was already beginning to explore the notion of attaining glory through some variety of suicide, of rendering death beautiful by taking it into your own hands, by giving yourself a past—a legend that signifies—rather than a future. Even then Scott was on his way to making himself a failure artist, working in the medium of grief.

So finally, I thought, I'd found him, or the first sign of what he was going to become. I suppose he could have ended up like my grandfather. He might have objected that his family was already on the downward slope while the Griggs were still living on Summit Avenue. But the Griggs were also in their descent. They just didn't know it. And now I'm here as the residue of Spengler's law of decline. The difference was one of degree, temperament, and illusion. Even as a boy Scott was looking back into the past while my grandfather imagined the prospects before him.

Other than that, they were alike in so many ways: they both had a romantic and sentimental view of women, family, and friendship and became uxorious husbands, diligent genealogists, and keepers of scrapbooks and correspondence. They made notes about everything that transpired in their lives and, in my grandfather's case, took thousand of photographs. College was probably the great watershed of their histories, and perhaps the one great difference between them was that my grandfather became a "Yale man" and remained one. Hanging near the well-stocked bar in his basement den was a picture of him holding a football, grinning around the time of his seventieth birthday, with the caption "Yale '16; Still Carrying the Ball". Scott, by contrast, never graduated from his college and so, even if only to him, his credentials as a "Princeton man" were suspect and incomplete. And maybe on that account, he remained fixed in the past, stuck fast in his junior year. He had gotten into "a good school" but didn't finish the job. The laws of St. Paul Academy may be every bit as iron as those of Marx, Hegel, and Spengler.

That's not to say that my grandfather did not contemplate and even revel in his own past. But his vision was nostalgic rather than tragic. He could examine the past and laugh or shrug or even weep, but then, like a scrapbook, he could close it and put it away.

I suppose that may mean that he never comprehended it as Scott had and that his perspective might be called superficial or sentimental. Surely the World War I of Scott's imagination was more terrible than the real war my grandfather experienced, even with its screaming wounded and severed limbs. My grandfather was satisfied with a certain banality in that regard. He did not try to make art of the past or of himself. But perhaps he knew that to go there deeply, entirely, perfectly—deliberately—you have to die. And that, I think, is why he shook his head so heavily that day I asked him about him and Scott. It was not just that by dying at age forty-four Scott had died before his time, but that he had been dead already for a long while.

≈

I'm fourteen years older than Fitzgerald was at his death. That is not particularly old, but at the same time death is no longer a theoretical possibility for me but an incipient fact: I have, at age fifty-eight, more of a past than I do a future.

We're told it's not a good thing to think too much about this, to "dwell" on death. But it is among the dead that we do dwell. They built the better part of the world we inhabit—its history, culture, points of pride, and grudges—and our existence is entirely contingent on theirs: we were conceived through their eros and their hope. Their flesh became our flesh; the tinder of their spirit ignited ours. Their monuments are all around us, our own selves among them.

It's all too easy—at least it has been for me—to see the world as a graveyard; to miss the vital truth that while, we share the world with the dead, we, too, have some business here. Like the thirteen-year-old Scott's John Sanderson, we live in debt to the dead, but we repay it by keeping ourselves alive, by tending their habitations, which are our home too.

Art is contingent on imagination, and if you have an especially active imagination, as Fitzgerald certainly did, you see the past more deeply and intently than other people. You may see ghosts, and eventually see them more than you see the living, and you may begin to see yourself among them. Their world—your need to be in it, to sustain and be sustained by it—is more real than the actual world: the past becomes present.

I was trying to keep these things—absence and presence—in balance, to honor and love the past, Scott and Ben, while continuing to live among the living. And I began to feel that going too deep into memory and art —at least for me—*was* morbid, the one leading to a directionless grief and the other to a hollow aestheticism, a preoccupation with specters and surfaces.

But I needed to look into two more things. The first was Scott's "Thoughtbook", a kind of diary he kept in 1910 and early 1911, just after he'd published "A Debt of Honor" in *Now and Then*. His spelling is poor (a life time affliction) and his handwriting is crabbed and clumsy in the manner of a fourteen-year-old, stagy with flamboyant serifs and capitals. It looks like my handwriting at that age, like any boy's I suppose, and the events it transcribes are banal. The entries are mostly about the other kids Scott knows, about who he likes and who likes him, about who is most popular, and especially about the girls Scott has crushes on and whether they like him back. There was Violet Stockton:

> …She had some sort of book called flirting
> by sighns and Jack and I got it away from
> Violet and showed it too all the boys. Violet
> got very mad and went into the house. I got
> very mad and therfor *I* went home…*I just
> hate Violet*.

Scott transferred his affections to Margaret Armstrong, but that, too, ended in tragedy at my grandfather's house:

> One Saturday night about two weeks later
> my finish came. We were over at Ben
> Grigg's, four boys, Reub, Ben, Ted & I, and
> four girls Margaret, Marie, Elizabeth &
> Dorothy & that evening Margaret got an
> awful crush on Reuben which at the time I
> write this is still active.

That is the end of the "Thoughtbook". And for a time thereafter, Scott later recorded in his *Ledger*, he 'became desperately holy".

That seems to have been the last time religion mattered to him. He went to mass a few times at Princeton, and when he died he was denied a Catholic burial on account of having been out of communion for such a long time. But my path and his had crossed in a church: back in St. Paul one Christmas Eve after college, Scott, having gotten more than a little tight at a dinner-party, "felt religion descend upon me…A warm current seemed to run through my body. My sins were washed away and I felt, as my host drained a drop or so from the ultimate bottle, that my life was beginning all over again."

He went to the Episcopal church a block behind his parents' house on Summit Avenue, St. John the Evangelist. He began looking for a friend in the brimming pews with whom he might sit and, searching the congregation, weaved up the aisle towards the pulpit. There he met the eyes of the rector, said, "Don't mind me, go on with the sermon", and turned around and headed back down the aisle and out the door.

St. John's was my grandparents church, the church where they and my mother and father were married, where the Griggs had a family pew, second row on the left, directly behind the spot where Scott stood during his drunken outburst. At the same age as Scott was when he began his "Thoughtbook", I, too, became "desperately holy". I was baptized, confirmed, and served as an altar boy in that same church, under the gaze of the white stone angel whose hands held the font. Scott must have stumbled past her as he approached the pulpit that Christmas Eve. I spent hundreds of hours in that church, and I still think of sitting in my grandfather's pew, on Christmas Eve, a soft persistent snow falling outside like the tolling of a bell. I wrote a scene, set precisely there, in my first novel, of a patrician family daydreaming at midnight mass as the life they think is theirs by right, unbeknownst to them, is crumbling away.

Scott seems to have felt he had desecrated a holy place that Christmas Eve. He memorialized that night in a piece called "The Most Disgraceful Thing I Ever Did" written a year after he'd left St. Paul for good. For me, St. John's was only holy in the way it had been for him, as a repository of memory and yearning, the warm burrow of an imagined past. It had nothing much to do with mercy or God. the altar candles are guttering and will leave a terrible darkness.

I still wanted to look at one last thing connected to Scott and Ben: my grandfather's boyhood photo album. It's exactly contemporaneous with Scott's "Thoughtbook", and there they all are, in their knickerbockers and caps and pinafores and hair-bows, at Summit Avenue and Dellwood: Reuben, Ben, and Ted, and Margaret, Marie, Elizabeth, and Dorothy. It's only Scott who's not present, for whatever reason. Was he simply not around when my grandfather was taking pictures or did my grandfather exclude him, perhaps out of some kind of contempt—there might have been that, too, in the shaking of his head seventy-five years later—or a preconscious sense that Scott was, yes, a failure?

I've never been able to escape either Scott or Ben: when I render the account of my own life up to now, perhaps what was true of Scott is true of me. I've attained neither my grandfather's well-earned contentment nor Scott's hard-earned genius, neither their angels nor their demons.

Better to imagine that I simply took a different course, my own path, the one I needed to follow to find myself. We were very big on finding ourselves when I was the age that Scott was at Princeton; and I suppose it came, as our parents had said all along, to no more than following our immediate desires and inclinations. I was going to be a painter, then a filmmaker, then an academic and public intellectual, and, finally, a writer. Coming from St. Paul, Minnesota, from the milieu of Summit Avenue and St. Paul Academy, with a tender and elegiac conception of love, of winters long ago and all the dying falls, and of childhood and youth, I knew against whom I must take the measure of myself. And as things stand, I have failed. Scott and Zelda knew what it took: it takes everything.

My grandfather knew all this about me from my childhood and adolescence. That day a dozen years ago, shrouded in his oxblood robe, shaking his head, he foresaw the rest. As for Scott, his story was no more than an alternate life to my grandfather's own—tragedy instead of comedy—which a neighborhood boy he had once known had chosen.

Perhaps it took no great wisdom or experience to understand this about me. Maybe that girl at Dellwood had known, had telegraphed to me, by the slightest rotation of her tanned shoulder cupped in a candy-heart pink shift, that, yes, as Scott had written in *Tender is the Night*, "all the old things are true," that my fears were facts.

Scott himself wrote that "my finish came" one night in the Griggs' parlor in 1911. It was just a pretty girl, but it was always a pretty girl with Scott. So it really was all over then, and the rest of his life was mere phantasm, a ghost writing his memoir, over and over again. People in St. Paul, my grandfather among them, were losing track of him. It seems to me now, as I prepare to put both him and Ben aside—to save myself as best I can, to find some mercy—that at age fourteen Scott was already Dick Diver, a walking, breathing absence. Scott had written of Dick's disappearance and uncertain whereabouts at the very end of *Tender is the Night*:

> Dick opened an office in Buffalo, but evidently without success...a few months later that he was in a little town named Batavia, New York, practising general medicine, and later that he was in Lockport, doing the same thing...his latest note was post-marked from Hornell, New York, which is some distance from Geneva and a very small town; in any case he is almost certainly in that section of the country, in one town or another.

I too am a wanderer, less in the manner of Dick Diver than of Fitzgerald himself; or, rather, a kind of aesthetic tourist who takes his inspiration from Fitzgerald and his ilk. I have been to every address in Paris that Fitzgerald (and Hemingway too) occupied during the 1920s, and I tracked down the villa on the Cote d'Azur upon which Dick Diver's was modeled. I've gone to England, Germany, Austria, and Italy on the track of other writers and artists. Sometimes, standing across the street from one or another house or apartment, I feel conspicuous. I wonder if I've been observed by the current occupants of the property and if I seem suspicious: if I'll be confronted and asked the nature of my business, something I doubt I could explain.

6.

BAYHAM STREET

This is the last thing.

I had a sister whom I hardly knew, whose existence I might doubt entirely if it were not for some photographs that show us together. I can see her, you might say, in my mind's eye, but only in one dimension: I'm not sure I can say what she "was like", how her features, bearing, and voice seemed in their entirety. Up to a point, I might have been able to piece her together—to imagine, if not a story, at least a character—through the photographs. But a photograph is no more than a refraction of a moment that nothing other than a lens ever saw, scarcely a pinprick in the fabric that veils a life. A photograph seems to contain and to mean much more than that, but perhaps what it does most of all is to induce longing, a hunger for everything— the day and the persons and the place—that it does not contain and which are irretrievably lost to us.

So sensing, perhaps, that it was a dead end, that it would end in bafflement and frustration, I didn't pursue the trail of this sister I'd scarcely even met—I haven't even bothered to mention her name, Patty. But someone sent me another photograph. When my grandparents' house was cleared out, their books were donated to the local library and, sifting through the cartons, a librarian found a photo album. She knew my name and sent it to me.

It was a tiny thing, the pages just big enough to hold one small photo of each of my siblings, my cousins, and me. It had belonged to my grandmother, and I'd seen pretty much every photo in it, these having been widely circulated among the family—every photo but one, that of a little girl, perhaps four years old, in a green dress on a red sofa against a green wall.

She has a fierce look, of insouciance and even defiance. Her arms are crossed in a kind of resigned impatience. She could not care less and yet she insists that you pay attention to her. I thought I knew who it was—the album contained nothing but my grandmother's grandchildren—but the little girl's demeanor threw me off. This child wasn't anything like what I had understood or had remembered Patty to be.

I sent the picture to my other sister, who's five years older than I and was two years Patty's senior. She didn't recall seeing it before, but she confirmed that it was our sister: Patty, who had been diagnosed as mentally retarded when she was two and confined to an institution; who was put (unlike me and my sister) into my father's custody when my parents divorced; who subsequently developed into a child with normal psychological and cognitive functioning; and who died—by then a bright and vivacious young woman—in a head-on collision during her second year of college.

Her transformation had been dramatic, even miraculous, and no one ever explained quite how it came about. There'd been a psychiatrist in Boston, a Dr. Fleming, but beyond the fact that someone had done some sort of therapy with Patty, the secret, as the cliché says, died with her. But by all reports she was someone else entirely as an infant and small child or, rather, she was almost no one at all. I was an infant then, but my sister remembers Patty's visits home from the institution. She wanted to play with Patty the way a big sister should play with her little sister. But Patty wouldn't play. She sat. Or sat and stared. Sometimes she said strange or incomprehensible things. She said "kalifidos", by which my sister eventually figured out she meant "cowboy".

Other people had reported similar things: she was slow, vacant, abstracted. And there were other photos that seemed to corroborate that view. In her baby pictures, she's doughy, ill defined, never quite roused from sleep. In a later photo, she's about two, and she's standing in front of a mirror trying to comb her hair. She's smiling avidly, as if she's amusing herself by combing the hair of this *other* child, the one she sees in the mirror. Either way, she's been photographed unawares—unlike any of her other childhood photos—and, also uniquely, she's smiling. She thinks she's alone, just her and perhaps this other little girl who lives in the mirror. And so she is happy.

That photo was taken on one of Patty's visits home from her institution. My mother and father were still living together, although their marriage was disintegrating. And perhaps Patty—the shame and worry and disappointment of her—was a factor, a shadow cast over their happiness, a vacuum that deprived them of oxygen, that caused the flame between them to die. In any case, it was said that my mother couldn't cope with Patty or, for that matter, very much else.

In fact the most specific explanation any of us ever heard for Patty's condition had to do with my mother, with something she had done or failed to do for this daughter of hers. Part of the vagueness and mystery surrounding the matter attaches to the fact that none of us is quite sure with whom the story originated. But the gist of it was that my mother had caused Patty to withdraw, to hide or disappear, to annihilate herself.

There's one more photo that perhaps bears out something like this. She's looking at the camera, or at a person near the camera. Her mouth is slightly open, the upper lip just arched upward as though she's about to speak or is beginning to register some surprise. As in the other photos, she's wearing a smocked dress and here she has a little purse slung over her shoulder. But this grown-up accessory doesn't delight her as the comb did in the other photograph: it looks like it's been pasted on her. Alongside the purse, her arm is stretched out, underside up, as though someone's about to draw blood from it. You come to her eyes last, despite the fact that they're dark, shiny, perhaps terrified. They're plangent, but somehow lack the capacity or will to cry. They're bright but stony, anthracite, obsidian. She's terrified or dead or, rather, she's as afraid of dying as she is of living.

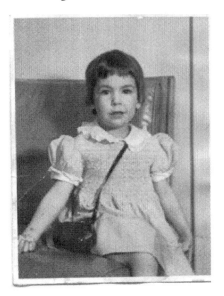

I first heard the idea that my mother was the author of Patty's condition when I was perhaps thirteen. Just then, I'd been reading Freud—more accurately, popularizations of Freud—and it seemed quite reasonable to me that a mother might do this to a child, or wish to (and in the Freudian cosmology wishing and doing were much the same thing): it was within a mother's powers of oppression and repression, active or passive, to crush a child or cause her to disappear into herself.

Anyway, it went without saying in the years between, say, 1955 and 1965, that Patty's affliction was at least in large part my mother's fault, and that my mother would, of course, herself appreciate this fact—she'd majored in child psychology in college—and be ashamed of it. Even without knowing quite why and how, she'd victimized this little girl, and she'd driven her husband away, or he'd left in disgust.

But that is not what struck me in the photograph I'd been sent. Far from being diffident or passive, she is intense, maybe even angry. She dominates the frame that encloses her and the colors that ought to subsume her. Her presence is such that she might almost come out of the photograph, thrust herself before you, and spit "kalifidos" in your face.

But, as someone pointed out right away, more than anything, she looks like me, like a shard of my family, like all of us who survived her, who persisted here after she was gone.

≈

I received that photo in the mail perhaps three years ago, and although I felt the imposition, the demand it seemed to make every time I looked at it, I did nothing about it. My other sister, however, was going to pursue the matter: she, after all, had known Patty. She lived in Massachusetts where Patty had spent most of her life, and she would look into her case. I, meanwhile, was chasing down other things, all of them missing or lost. I went to Bayham Street instead.

Charles Dickens lived on Bayham Street, Camden Town, London, in 1822, age ten, in a house of yellow brick. And there, staring out the window of "the little back garret," commenced the worst period of his life. On account of his family's penury, he was pulled out of school and put to work ten hours a day in a blacking factory under Hungerford Bridge. His father was thrown into the debtor's prison at Marshalsea. Charles lived on Bayham Street scarcely a year—his family moved constantly in order to evade their creditors—but it was the first place he lived in London and in some ways the last; in his imagination, he seemed to inhabit it for the rest of his days.

It was definitively the house of the Cratchits in *A Christmas Carol* and of Mr. Micawber in *David Copperfield*. The view from the garret window of the dome of St. Paul's shrouded in smoke and fog is surely Pip's first vision of London in *Great Expectations*. I felt that in that garret, ashamed, oppressed by his child labor, and half-orphaned, that Dickens took his emptiness, the void that he might have become, and began to make it into art. I wanted to see where this had happened, to see what traces of it might still persist.

I went to London three times over the next two years and on each trip I went to Bayham Street. It's an ugly, straight swatch of row houses, flats, and public housing projects running south from Camden Town underground station. The first time I walked down one side of Bayham Street to its terminus at Crowndale Road—perhaps three-quarters of a mile—and back up the other side, looking for the blue plaque that marks buildings with historical and literary associations in London. But there were no plaques on Bayham Street. It seemed impossible that anyplace in London connected with Dickens wasn't marked in this fashion, least of all his first boyhood home in the city. Perhaps I'd made a mistake about the name of the street.

At home I rechecked the address, and when I returned to London six months later I brought the house number with me. I now knew the address was 16 Bayham Street. But though there were dozens of small brick houses of early nineteenth century vintage, none of them corresponded to that address. There was no number 16 and no blue plaque, either. It occurred to me that perhaps the house had stood on the site of one the vast blocks of public housing flats—built, it seemed, in the 1960s or 70s—at the south end of the street, and that in their construction both the houses, the address, and the blue plaque might have vanished. Perhaps I was the only person who had any interest in finding or seeing the house; perhaps I was the only person who understood how important that place had been. And in this thought I took a sort of melancholy pride. But either way, I had to accept that neither the house nor the place where it stood seemed to exist.

The next time I came to London, in the spring of 2005, I had no plans to visit Bayham Street. I'd spent the previous five days in Germany walking for six hours a day, and thanks to a pair of ill-fitting shoes my feet were almost bloody with abrasions and blisters. I was stopping in London for twenty hours to catch my breath and wait until my flight home left the next day.

That next morning I went to Gower Street in Bloomsbury to shop for books. The Dickens had lived on Gower Street after vacating 16 Bayham Street, after Charles' father had been sent to Marshalsea. I wasn't moved by this fact—I think I'd forgotten it just then—but by a sense almost of dereliction, of having left something that ought to be done undone. So, with a plane to catch in a little over two hours, I took the tube to Camden Town.

I walked quickly over to Bayham Street and started down the west side, no number 16 and no blue plaques visible anywhere. In the distance I could see the end of the street at Crowndale Road, and I asked myself if I was really going to walk the whole way down, if I really needed to repeat this pointless trek in its entirety a third time. I had a plane to catch and a ten-hour flight to endure, so I compromised. I walked another block to where the modern housing projects began—the point beyond which there were no nineteenth century buildings—and crossed over to the east side of the street. I swear I surveyed every façade of every house between there and the Underground station, but I found nothing at all.

I went back to my hotel, got my bag, and rode the train to the airport. I was angry that I'd wasted yet more of my limited time abroad on Bayham Street, but at the same time I felt a kind of guilt, a sense that if I had only tried harder or looked more carefully I would have found Dickens' house. And as stupid and futile as I knew the impulse was, there was no other solution to my disappointment—to ease the longing, to complete the quest—than to go back to Bayham Street another time on another trip.

The next time, I was disappointed even before I got to London. I'd been in Italy for six weeks and then in Germany for a few days afterward. I'd gone to Germany specifically to visit Dresden and then Weimar. From the reading I'd done and the music I listened to, it came to seem to me that for one-hundred and fifty years— from the late eighteenth through the first third of the twentieth century—Germany possessed perhaps the most brilliant philosophic, scientific, and creative minds in the western world. Then, in scarcely a decade, it descended into the deepest barbarity humankind has ever known. This is a now commonplace observation. It wasn't entirely clear to me whether it described a paradox or a necessary relation, an inevitability, but I wanted to see the evidence for it for myself.

For me Weimar and Dresden represented the poles of that history. Bucolic, cobbled, park-like Weimar was the home of Goethe and the Romantic movement, Germany's intellectual and literary heart, and the site of the foundation of its last democratic government before Hitler. Dresden, the baroque capital of the kingdom of Saxony, had once been called "Florence on the Elbe". It was a center of German music and opera and an artists' colony that sheltered Schumann, Wagner, Ibsen, Caspar David Friedrich, and Dostoevsky. Its museums had been the best in Germany, and they contained, among other masterpieces, Raphael's "Sistine Madonna", the painting that the nineteenth century considered the most beautiful art work in the world. In the final months of World War II, Dresden and perhaps 50,000 of its inhabitants were incinerated in a firestorm of Allied bombing, the greatest conflagration in the western theater of the war. Whether portrayed as an act of slaughter and destruction unjustified by any military need or as a well-deserved retribution for Nazi horrors, the annihilation of Dresden seemed to me to mark the final extinction of the German genius and civilization born at Weimar.

In Dresden, I'd checked into a post-modern edifice called the ArtHotel. My room was elegantly spare, decorated in black, gray, and blond wood. It overlooked the city soccer stadium, the assembly point over which the British bombers fanned out on their incendiary runs sixty years before. You would not know that from looking at it, or by turning in the opposite direction, to the southeast, where the bombs fell. Excepting the city's reconstructed baroque churches and palaces, most of the buildings in Dresden were erected after 1950. The more appealing among them are in the mode of the ArtHotel, but the majority are examples of Soviet Modernism from the era of the German Democratic Republic. The rubble and ruins have been completely vanquished, but a vista of empty form imposed on a waste ground—the ash meadow, the field sown with salt—stands in their place.

But it was ruins, or the remnants of them, I had come to see. I wanted to see cinders and scorched bricks, a baroque statue, perhaps decapitated or armless, tilted at an impossible angle but still standing on a darkling field of debris, a waft of phosphorous on the air. I wanted, if not the dead themselves, the places in which they died, the stage upon which their holocaust had been acted out.

There are a host of stories about the horror of the firestorm and its aftermath, any of which might drive anyone, man or child, mad, unspeakable things that might turn you to stone were you to see them: cellars, for example packed with asphyxiated, bloated corpses of mothers and children, inside which recovery workers could scarcely keep their footing on account of the carpet of maggots covering the floors. During the bombing, Dresdeners instinctively took shelter there, but the updraft of the firestorm outside literally sucked the oxygen from the basements.

The air temperature rose into the hundreds of degrees. Many people fled to the bank of the Elbe and immersed themselves in the water. Others tried to evade the heat by hiding in water tanks and fountains. But as the air temperature increased, the water in the fountains heated as well. Those who sheltered in them were boiled alive and then the water itself evaporated, leaving their corpses beached in the empty pools.

There is a photograph I came across that illustrates this phenomenon, and while I found it moving—it shows that there was literally nowhere to go, no escape from the firestorm—I suppose it also exercised a morbid fascination upon me. The fountain was in the Altmarkt or close by it, and I spent some hours scouring the area looking for it in the same hopeful and frustrated manner I'd searched Bayham Street, and to no more avail.

All that, seemingly every trace, has been erased. The past had been carted away, leveled, and paved over. It was not simply that there was no sign of it, no ruins or reminders, but that even the presence of the past had been obliterated: even the absence of what once was had been taken away. The past is, of course, dead, but here it had apparently never lived.

That evening, my feet sore from the day's futile reconnaissance, I ate alone in my hotel's chic dining room. For whatever reason—a lack of out-of-town visitors or few locals accustomed to dining out—the room seemed a stylish void, its grey walls too gray, the light a little too stark. The waiter stood nervously behind the bar or disappeared into the shelter of the kitchen. Music—the forlorn ranting of Leonard Cohen—echoed from the sound system. I felt lonely and grieving. I missed my family. I missed everyone I'd ever known, or known of.

The next morning I went to see the Sistine Madonna, the painting that transfixed the nineteenth century, the golden age of the annihilated Germany that once existed nowhere as much as in Dresden. It had been secreted underground outside the city and so survived the firestorm.

I hoped to either love it as much as Dostoevsky or disdain it as had Ruskin, or at least try to see some of what the past—the dead of one-hundred-fifty years ago—had seen in it. If nothing else, unlike Dresden, it was present, intact. There's a round banquette placed just in front of the painting, and you can sit before it like a fire or an altar. So I did.

You know it, this painting. Or rather you at least know *them*: the indolent and resigned putti at the bottom of the frame. To us, that tranche of the Sistine Madonna is almost an artwork in its own right and—to judge by its constant reproduction on calendars, posters, and consumer what-not—as much a talisman of art in the late twentieth/early twenty-first century, as the entire painting was in the nineteenth. And what makes this image iconic for us is the obvious fact that these angels are a couple of comedians, wiseacres and ironists. The curtains on either side of the frame have been pulled back to reveal Mary, her baby, and their papal attendants. It's—if you will—"The Madonna Show" and those little guys are the stagehands. They're not impressed, they've seen it before, and they're waiting for it to be over. These putti are cute but knowing, even hip. In their recognition of what's happening they're recognizably us, of our time.

You might say that what the putti—these moderns with wings—are commenting on is precisely what the nineteenth century loved about this painting: its notion of beauty as spectacle, as a parting of the curtains to reveal a view of the divine, of heaven. The Madonna and her attendants are standing on clouds, and they, too, are a little vaporous, particularly the Madonna herself whose tender beauty is somehow unboundaried, as though diffusing the light she contains. In truth, she was, to me, a little vague, not quite present. But the nineteenth century loved words like "diaphanous" and "effusion" and perhaps it loved this painting for so embodying them. For me, however, the Madonna's compassion and illumination did not so much shine as leak from her, puddling in a watery sweetness.

For all that, she seemed to me the first emphatically real historic presence I'd encountered in Dresden. She wasn't a replica, a reproduction, or a symbol of something missing or lost. But she also wasn't particular to this place. She could project herself—her facticity as art—anywhere. But I had come here to find genuine traces of something I felt I needed to comprehend, markers that were more than symbols or plaques or monuments. I wanted, if not the flames of the firestorm, a whiff of their smoke, a sign of their onetime presence here.

I ate a delicious piece of lemon cake in the reconstructed baroque café near the reconstructed opera house on whose site Wagner and Richard Strauss had premiered their works. I began walking back to the ArtHotel and it was snowing, turning darker and colder. The weather was coming in from the north and the east, from Poland and Russia, from the taiga and the steppes, the deep primal backyard—the shadow self, perhaps— Germany had so many times tried to enslave or destroy.

The avenue that led back to the hotel cut through what had been the royal precincts of the electors of Saxony, the princes who had made this place "Florence on the Elbe". Along one side were several office and apartment blocks from the GDR and along the other, stretching at least one or more blocks was a vacant lot, a thicket of trees, brush, and abandoned refuse and junk. At its far corner, jutting out from the tangle of bare trees and shrubs, huddled in the east wind and its scattershot of snow, stood the façade of what once must have been a small but imposing building.

As I came closer, I saw there was an inscription over the portal in the center cut in early nineteenth century characters. It said "ORANGERIE". The gateway was barricaded and braced with wood, as were the windows and the doors to either side. The stone was covered in places with graffiti and posters, and otherwise cracked, pocked, and stained. It might have been due to weathering, subsidence, and vandalism, but also, given its placement directly on the bombers' track, from heat, flame, and shrapnel.

When the building was intact, it must have had an ornate glass carapace beneath which orange and lemon trees were cultivated. Amongst them, in the custom of the time, the elector and his court might have taken tea and imagined themselves on the Bay of Naples. Now the building was pathetic twice over, once as an architectural folly consecrated to growing oranges where oranges could not grow and now as the shabby remnant of once great but now deposed kingdom and culture. The portal was like the curtain of the Sistine Madonna, a hundred-and-fifty years ago opening onto an ersatz Eden, and today, as the gelid wind blew in from the east, onto a GDR barricade with an overgrown lot behind it.

It was too cold to linger, too cold in fact to go out for the rest of the day, and I was catching a train to Weimar the next morning. But in the night, I realized that the Orangerie was what I had come to Dresden to see, or that it was going to be the best I could do, a real sign, a ruined but intact presence of the firestorm and the world it had incinerated. In the morning, on the way to the station, I lugged my bag to the curb opposite and took a picture. The snow had turned to sleet and most of what had fallen yesterday was melting beneath a southwest wind, from the direction of Weimar and of Naples.

Weimar was, on its face, everything that Dresden failed to be. There were old burghers' houses, venerable squares, churchyards flocked by birds, and a long park that wended along the river to Goethe's summer cottage, that even empty suggested the presence of children, of little girls in pinafores and smocked dresses in some eternal golden past. But most of all there was the light, on that day blue and gold, and you might well imagine why Goethe had become fascinated by optics and the science of color; why, it was said, his last words on his death bed were "mehr licht"— "more light".

The town is built less of stone or brick than plaster and wood, and the predominant colors are pine green, a pale butter-yellow, and a deep amber, the hue of the German dying fall, a register removed from the olive, lemon, and russet of Italy. Goethe was, of course, the original northern European Italophile, the author of the verses Schubert set to music in praise of Italy as the antidote to Romantic longing and melancholy.

As the cradle of German Romanticism Weimar has, of course, a magnificent cemetery, a rolling cavern of conifers and vines. But then perhaps Weimar itself is one vast graveyard which we amicably share with benign ghosts, its muses and geniuses, the dead with whom—having not been annihilated by history and its fires—we live in a parallel dimension, just adjoining theirs.

I got lost in the cemetery and I didn't mind at all. I couldn't find my way out to the southeast exit I believed ought to lead to Nietzsche's house. At last I found a gate that gave onto a street of nineteenth century houses, the Victorian suburbs of Weimar. Nietzsche's house—or rather his sister's house where, frail and demented after his

nervous and physical collapse in Turin, he spent the last ten years of life—lay somewhere nearby. I found it on a busy road descending a hill, a garden sloping away from one side of it. It was a boxy, mansard-roofed house, its volume restricted as though by a corset. There was a fussy

conservatory porch on one side of it, and I supposed
Nietzsche must have been wheeled out here most days to
take a little sun. I supposed he stared out into the garden,
dozed and muttered to himself and drooled.

It's a mediocre house of brick, the epitome of the
upright bourgeois contentment that Nietzsche held in
deepest contempt. If there is any mercy, he never knew
where he was. Like Goethe, he'd taken shelter in Italy.
Two years before, I'd sought him there, in Turin. As is my
wont with the past and its inhabitants, I'd asked too much
of him.

This time, I, too, had come to Germany from Italy.
Before Dresden, I'd spent two months in Umbria, writing
and teaching American undergraduates. The town was
called Orvieto, and it is famous for a crisp white wine and
for its Duomo, which contains frescoes by Fra Angelico and
Signorelli. It's a big church for such a small town, owing to
two facts: that, on a high and secure plateau not far from
Rome, the medieval popes frequently took refuge here; and
also that it was the locus of the miracle of Bolsena, the
event that put the important feast of Corpus Christi on the
church calendar.

The miracle takes the substance and form of many such
stories—apocryphal hokum frothed up into transcendent
epiphany—and goes like this: It seems that a German
priest, Peter of Prague, stopped at Bolsena to say his daily
mass enroute to Rome. He was a good and pious priest, but
one who found it difficult to believe that Christ was actually
present in the consecrated Host. On that day, however, as
he said the words of the Consecration, blood began to seep
from the Host, to trickle over his hands, to drip onto the
altar and the corporal. The priest immediately went to
Orvieto, where the pope was then in residence, and the
authenticity of the miracle was confirmed. The feast was
officially instituted a year later.

I don't know how much this would have normally interested me: I am reserved and a bit cerebral in my Catholicism, which is in any case, pretty well attenuated these days. I find myself a little embarrassed by devotions of too sweaty and visceral sort, those involving relics, flaming hearts, tears, and, as here, blood. But in the miracle of Bolsena there was one more key figure besides Peter of Prague and Pope Urban IV: Thomas Aquinas. Thomas is, of course, *the* great Catholic theologian, utterly devout but rigorously intellectual. He marshaled, as much as anyone ever has, the reasons one ought to believe—the logic and system of God and his creation—and he's deepened, insofar as I understand him, my shallow faith. He's also "difficult" in the contemporary sense and, in my considerable vainglory, I like the feeling of belonging to the elite who try to take him on.

So I was intrigued to discover that Thomas had been involved in the affair of Bolsena; that he'd been in Orvieto at the time in 1263 and Urban had put him on the case, so to speak, as both an investigator of the miracle and the author of the liturgy in which the feast day was to be formalized. On further investigation, I learned that Thomas's residence in Orvieto was not a half a block from the apartment I was living in. Like Bayham Street and the hotels in Rome and Naples my grandfather had stayed in a hundred years ago that I'd also been trying to locate, this was a search, both archeological and intellectual, I had to undertake.

Thomas's home in Orvieto was on the present-day Piazza XXIX Novembre where my son had been playing soccer every day with the neighborhood kids. The piazza was dominated by a 1930's era building used as a military barracks but in one corner stood the church of San Domenico. I'd been looking at it as I oversaw Andrew's play in the center of the square. On its flank, adjacent to the barracks, the exterior wall of the nave showed signs of what once must have been another wing of the building just as tall as the rest of the church: the shadow of an enormous arch, of buttresses removed, of truncated columns, of an open space now sealed with stone. I spent some time trying to figure out what this signified. I went inside the church, both at mass (the parish was one of the most vibrant of the town) and afterwards, and what I saw inside was as confusing as the outside: columns with one side stripped away as though by a cleaver, and others whose feet didn't align with their trunks or that terminated half-way up the wall for no reason. More happily, there were also some signs of Thomas here: a patch of thirteenth century fresco and, more substantially, an oak box said to contain the chair in which he wrote, taught, and prayed.

In those two materials, the wood and the paint on the wall, Thomas was, I felt, still vaguely present in the church of San Domenico, although perhaps only he could tell you precisely to what extent and in what manner. Thomas's great preoccupation was the relation between the seen and the unseen, between things and their sources, between their material substance and the form in which they appear, contained in the flux of time and space. In this, he was attempting to fit the philosophical realism of Aristotle (whose writings had just been rediscovered by medievals) to Christian theology and revelation. You might say he was trying to square matter with spirit, no easy task, then or now.

Thomas was particularly well suited to investigate the miracle at Bolsena. What had transpired with Peter of Prague represented a momentary tear in the veil separating the physical and spiritual aspects of the sacrament of the Eucharist. One definition of a sacrament is "an outward and visible sign of an inward and invisible grace", but in this case the unseen—the actual transformation of bread and wine into Christ's body and blood—had become utterly tangible.

Admittedly, this notion of the "real presence" is one of the more difficult—not to say, for some, incredible—doctrines of the Church. Christians intuited it from Christ's words at the Last Supper ("This is my body"), but it was Thomas, with help from Aristotle, who worked out its underlying logic. Things, according to Aristotle, consist of substances and "accidents", their essential matter and the visible form in which that matter manifests itself. For example, you might say that ice, liquid water, and vapor are all accidents of the substance H_2O. In the Mass, the substances of bread and wine are transformed into Christ's body and blood while retaining their original outward accidents.

This is still a miracle—it transcends what seem to us the laws of science—but there's a kind of whole-hearted optimism in Thomas's thought: Created things are both real and good rather than defective or false. Thomas insisted on the real presence not only of the Eucharist but the real presence of objects and persons and therefore of their value, their worthiness to be attended and loved. For Thomas, Paul of Prague's inability to believe in the real presence was a refusal to see the reality of the real at its most profound, the indwelling of God in His creation.

To me, in Orvieto, it also seemed that Thomas must be insisting on his own presence—signs of himself—here and now that I might see. But I couldn't puzzle out the church of San Domenico, still less locate the place where Thomas had done his writing and thinking. Yet it was that trace of his presence that I really wanted to find. Meanwhile, I'd gone down to Rome to visit the Ambasciatori Palace Hotel where my grandfather had lodged some dozen times in the 1920s and 1930s.

The Ambasciatori had been remodeled three or four times since then, most recently in the nineties "nel rispetto dell'originaria fisionomia degli ambienti", "in keeping with the original appearance of the surroundings". But other than the grand staircase in the lobby, which might have contained some elements from eighty years ago, it seemed that not a single surface present in my grandfather's time had survived.

In 1934 he'd brought my father with him here as a young adolescent. Apparently the Ambasciatori Palace had not impressed my father either. In a letter home on hotel stationary he only complained that "I don't like speagete" and that "I never can understand what they are talking about when they try to tell us what there is to eat". He also wrote that he hoped to see Mussolini "some day when he comes out of his house", although I never knew if this wish was granted. He can't understand the things he wants to know. He can't see what he wants to see. He's unmistakably my father, and Patty's father too.

That same year, Mussolini had been at work in Orvieto, and what he did there had a bearing on the Piazza XXIX Novembre and the church of San Domenico. As in other such regimes, the Italian fascists promoted "physical culture"—a cult of the body founded on notions of the

Italian nation and race—and they wanted to establish an "Accademia Femminile di Educazione Fisica", a woman's athletic academy. The chosen location was Orvieto and the building then occupying the prospective construction site was the church of San Domenico and its cloister.

I'd learned this after my return from Rome and the Ambasciatori. Our apartment was in a palazzo belonging to an elderly couple who were natives of Orvieto. Signora Petinelli was an elegant woman in her late sixties, a skilled cook and a font of Orvietan history and culture going back to the middle ages. Her husband, "il dottore", was a nattily dressed retired surgeon and art connoisseur who, that autumn, recited Catullus in Latin as he gave me a flu shot.

They knew all about San Domenico and the Accademia Femminile: It had all happened while they were children living in this neighborhood. A controversial project at the time, it pitted civic boosters who welcomed the largesse from Rome against preservationists and clergy and congregation of San Domenico. The fascists and the

ORVIETO – LA CHIESA DI SAN DOMENICO PRIMA DEL 1931

boosters won out, of course but, in a sop to the parish, a portion of the church was allowed to stand. The entire nave—the church's larger, main axis in which the congregation sat—was demolished and the transept—the church's shorter, smaller crossing axis—was transformed into a nave with a new altar at one end. The truncated pillars I'd seen inside and outside were the scars from the amputation of the original nave.

Until then San Domenico had consisted not only of the church but of gardens, a dormitory, a cloister, and a refectory where the brothers—among them Thomas—worked, ate, and slept. All that was gone, save for the rump of the transept. It did not seem enough, not as much as I wanted of Thomas's residual presence, of real signs of the reality of the great architect of realism, of the real presence.

Any Orvietan over the age sixty-five could probably have told me what I'd wanted to know. But I didn't speak Italian well enough to form the question or, without several slow repetitions, to understand the answer. More crucially, I felt driven—perhaps almost to the point of obsession--to use only the evidence of my own eyes, however uninformed my capacity to perceive the reality of the things I was looking at. I was twice blind, both to words and to the realities of things seen and unseen.

Sigmund Freud, I later learned, had also been to Orvieto. In fact, he based the first chapter of one of his key works, *The Psychopathology of Everyday Life*, on an incident connected to Orvieto's duomo, the great church raised in response to the revelation of the real presence to Peter of Prague. On a train, Freud wanted to talk about the frescoes in the duomo, but he could not for the life of him recall the name of one of their two principal creators—Signorelli—despite having seen them on several visits. Analyzing this inexplicable lapse of memory, Freud recollected that just prior to his attempt to talk about the frescoes, he had been preoccupied with the suicide of one of his patients whose problems Freud traced to "an incurable sexual disturbance", undoubtedly homosexuality. He decided that the troubling nature of these thoughts—of sexuality and death—had caused him to forget the name of Signorelli, and upon this incident Freud subsequently formulated one of his principal discoveries, repression.

The notion that wishes, intentions, and purposes run deep within us like underground rivers is key to Freud's view of the soul. We both know and do not know what we are doing, and repression is the device whereby we square that contradiction. It's what enabled that unknown diagnostician in the 1950s to conclude that my mother might both want to drive Patty mad—withdrawing her love in such a way that Patty in turn withdrew herself entirely from the world—and yet feel she would never, ever want to do such a thing to her child; that her maternal love was double-edged, that its presence was a kind of void into Patty might fall and disappear, consumed.

That is Freud in extreme form, Freud forgetting Signorelli's name almost as if he wished the Duomo frescoes destroyed. For me, in Orvieto, I can't say that I in some way avoided the facts I thought I wanted to know. But I would say that my own preoccupations and needs prevented me from finding what I sought, from hearing and seeing what was before me, from translating the words and images correctly. Sometimes things may indeed look or sound absurd but still in fact represent the truth. Sometimes kalifidos does mean cowboy.

To find what I wanted to find, I needed help, and Signora Petinelli gave it to me. Presence doesn't always make itself present simply because we desire it to be. And perhaps the presence we seek—however sure we are that it is other persons and things, the presence of the past—is actually our own presence, the reality of ourselves standing in relation to all reality, to the real presence. Maybe I needed the Thames, Bayham Street, Dresden, Weimar, Turin, and Rome for that purpose, and now Orvieto too.

I'd been a little dejected by the discovery of the almost total destruction of signs of Thomas Aquinas in Orvieto. Then, in scarcely an aside, Signora Petinelli mentioned there was a little more, "poche piccole tracce"—a few small traces--inside the academy, now the military barracks into which the priory had originally extended. She would try to get me inside: She knew people, calls could be made.

A few days later, Signora Petinelli knocked on our apartment door. Was I ready to go? She had talked to the commandante. We could come if we went right now. She and I walked down the block and across the piazza XXIX Novembre. Buttons were pushed, speakerphones addressed, and buzzers sounded. The metal gates swung open. A young officer escorted us through a vestibule and through a second gate.

We were outside again in a vast courtyard enclosed by walls in the same Mussolini-Modernist style as the façade, an arena in which I supposed the flower of fascist womanhood performed their calisthenics. But on one wall, along the bottom, something entirely different stood out in relief: an arcade—a series of open arches separated by Romanesque columns atop a wide level balustrade—of dark amber stone. It was a section of cloister, cut off above and on both sides and incorporated into the fourth fascist wall, left intact on an architect's whim or in a perverse attempt at recycling or cost-control or maybe because of some inchoate sense that, yes, the Accademia Femminile di Educazione Fisica ought to contain a little fragment of San Domenico.

"It's thirteenth century," Signora Petinelli said with confidence. That meant this was Thomas's cloister, that he would have worked and written here; would have paced circuits though this corridor and around the other three sides--now vanished—of the cloister.

Signore Petinelli was talking rapidly in Italian about Thomas and the priory, apparently for the officer's benefit. Most of what she was saying was going past me. I thought the officer could not possibly know whom she was talking about or take any interest in it, but it seemed that he did. He nodded assent or expressed surprise with genuine enthusiasm and curiosity. Or so it seemed to me, since he spoke English even more poorly than I spoke Italian.

As Signora Petinelli continued recounting the history of the priory, Corpus Christi, the real presence, and this *fratre*, *scrittore*, and *grande filosofo* who had lived just here three-quarters of a millennium ago, I simply stood looking at the stratum of cloister frozen in Mussolini's wall. This, somehow, was the trace of Thomas I had been after, the real presence of him, caught unmistakably here. And to record and mark it--just to make sure of what I was seeing-- I wanted to take a picture.

As soon as I lifted my camera, the officer raised his hand and gestured an emphatic "no". Signora Petinelli protested that surely there was no harm in photographing an old section of wall. But it was absolutely forbidden, the officer said apologetically. No photography whatsoever was permitted in a military installation. He turned to me and spoke half in Italian, half in English. Surely I understood the reasons, after "il undici Settembre". "All this must stay...lost, secret," he said.

So there could be no photo. I would have to accept what I had seen on faith, to keep it present before my eyes through trust and hope. Once past the gate, I did take a picture of the children--Andrew's soccer friends--on the piazza, and they, present there, will have to stand as the outward sign of what is inside, of what Thomas and his God are making real, putting us in the presence of, realizing in and through us.

When I came back from Italy, Weimar, Dresden, and London, I hoped there might be some word about my sister Patty. We'd tracked down her psychiatrist, Doctor Fleming, who had apparently effected or at least witnessed her transformation. But we were too late. After a distinguished career at Massachusetts General, Children's Hospital, the Judge Baker Clinic, and Harvard Medical School, she'd died four years before at the age of 89.

We'd also tried to locate Patty's medical records. Someone in our family had dimly remembered that there was supposed to have been a case history published that was based on her. The name had been changed but we would surely recognize her by the details. I went to the medical school library near my home and scavenged the indexes and databases. I found two articles by Doctor Fleming, one on a medication used in the treatment in schizophrenia, the other on the families of juvenile offenders. Neither had anything to do with Patty.

The hunt for medical records was still continuing. All the institutions Patty's doctor had been associated with were helpful, but one by one they reported they had found nothing. Perhaps Doctor Fleming had treated Patty as a private patient, in which case a relative might know the location of her papers. But Doctor Fleming had left no survivors, and it seemed unlikely that files and paperwork from forty years past would have survived her.

So my family and I are left where we began, with the vague impressions and hunches of people now dead that we heard speak long ago, of whom our own memories have begun to fade. My mother was already gone. She spent the last year of her life in a nursing home, all the day lying flat on her back with her hands folded over her stomach, staring at the ceiling and now and again dozing off. She'd laid herself out like a corpse. When she did die, without so much as a gasp, just before dawn on a morning in March, it took the nurse and orderly some time to realize she'd undergone any alteration at all.

I wish I'd asked her about Patty. But neither I or my other sister had ever devised a way to bring up the subject without it leading to a discussion of Patty's specific pathology and thence, inevitably to my mother's part in it; to her role as the "rejecting" or "emotionally absent" mother who induced "infantile schizophrenia" in her child, as surely as if she'd throttled her or scalded her with boiling water. Looked upon now from an age less certain of Freud's intuitions on repression and unconscious wishes—of the inexplicable absence in the mind of a name connected to a fresco cycle in a church in Orvieto—it seems a little too dramatic, too determined to find the fatal deeds and outsized personalities of the Greek tragedies Freud loved in a smallish mock-Tudor bungalow in the Midwest of the early 1950s. I suppose that in practical terms it's also a calumny on my mother that provides an answer to the mystery of Patty at the cost of raising, for me, an unacceptable question.

So barring that explanation, here is what I know about Patty: she was born, she vanished into a state a little like autism or retardation or catatonia, she reemerged as a person pretty much like anyone else, and then she died. She was not here, then she was here, and then she was gone again: absence, presence, absence. "He's here and he's not here. He's there and he's not there," Garroway had said in 1957. "He brings a bell or he doesn't bring a bell." When I saw the kinescope of that moment last year, it made me weep.

Maybe that appearing and disappearing is an aspect of Nietzsche's eternal recurrence, the momentary blackness where the loop of film was spliced, the gap between repetitions of the same scenes. Patty died in a cataclysmic head-on car crash, exactly as Bob died. You can argue that she was entirely innocent, blameless in the causation of her death, and that he, drunk and sexually aroused, was not. But surely we are all innocent at that moment, just for that one instant.

I wonder what it was like, Patty's and the other car hurtling towards one another, fusing, separating, and coming to rest, steaming, burning, then exhausted. After the alarm, the terror, perhaps the flare of images as every instant of her life—the secret, hidden parts none of us ever saw—passed through her mind's eye, what happened, where was she?. As the impact came, as she dove into the firestorm, through that veil that hung before her like the windshield toward which the oncoming car pressed, did she disappear? Did her soul and the soul of the old woman in the other vehicle wheel past one another, above the smoldering thicket of the wreck? When did she leave the scene, when was she no longer present there or in any other place to which we, the living, can go?

Thomas Aquinas said that the soul is "substantial form", an immaterial matter that shapes and integrates all the parts and aspects of the human person. A person is not a person without a soul or without a body, and it is the presence of this substantial form that makes a body a person rather than a corpse. I am not sure I know what Thomas meant by this, although I am sure he did. I wonder if it was necessary that every trace of life—like the cooling metal of the engine and the condensation of radiator water on the asphalt—be stopped and still before Patty's soul could take its leave. So perhaps she lingered in that place long after the state troopers arrived and the spinning red and blue lights were extinguished and the ambulances departed with their cargo.

I don't know. I can't see any sign of it. The picture of the soul—the psyche—I grew up with is closer to Freud's than Thomas', a chasm of fractured strata through which one descends into ever deepening and incomprehensible darkness, far from any unifying form, still less the presence of its creator. But faith—my faith and Thomas's, the one that I attempt to maintain a grasp upon despite the evidence of so much of my senses, the glaring absences that seem so often to make proofs—says it is otherwise: that Patty is present to God and God is present to her, not by signs or traces, memory or hope, but in fact, in full view. I would like someday, as Thomas described, for God to make me present to Himself, and to her, and to everything I thought was lost or missing.

I don't, of course, know how or if that will happen. I may go back to Bayham Street. After I came home, after it was clear there were no records, no signs or explanations of Patty—after I learned she might have been as imaginary as Little Dorrit or Miss Havisham; as real or unreal—I found out that Bayham Street had been renumbered late in the nineteenth century. Number 16 is now number 141. There is also, somewhere, a plaque, and I found a picture—a little hazy and ill focused—of it. It isn't blue at all. I am looking for the boy in the garret looking out onto the fulminating world, calculating how he might make his way in it, how he could leave a mark upon it that someone much later, someone like me, might find.

19581331R00098

Made in the USA
Lexington, KY
27 December 2012